This
book belongs to

_____

...a woman who delights
in God's wisdom.

God's Wisdom for a Woman's Life

Elizabeth George

HARVEST HOUSE™ PUBLISHERS

EUGENE, OREGON

Cover by Terry Dugan Design, Minneapolis, Minnesota

Cover photo © Dana Edmunds, Getty Images

Acknowledgment

As always, thank you to my dear husband, Jim George, M. Div., Th. M., for your able assistance, guidance, suggestions, and loving encouragement on this project.

For additional practical help, you'll want to obtain the supplemental volume *God's Wisdom for a Woman's Life Growth and Study Guide*.

GOD'S WISDOM FOR A WOMAN'S LIFE
Copyright © 2003 by Elizabeth George
Published by Harvest House Publishers
Eugene, Oregon 97402
www.harvesthousepublishers.com

Library of Congress Cataloging-in-Publication Data
   George, Elizabeth, 1944–
   God's wisdom for a woman's life / Elizabeth George.
        p. cm.
Includes bibliographical references.
   ISBN 0-7369-1061-1 (pbk.)
   1. Christian women--Religious life. I. Title.
      BV4527.G4592 2003
      248.8'43–dc21   2003005537

Printed in the United States of America.

03 04 05 06 07 08 09 10 / BP-KB / 10 9 8 7 6 5 4 3 2 1

Contents

Seeking a Heart of Wisdom

As one of God's women I'm sure your life is complex and demanding. You wear a multitude of hats, possess a long list of responsibilities, and are expected to live out your many God-given roles. On top of these assignments, you're also supposed to oversee your spiritual growth, to be a time-management expert, to take care of your appearance, to watch what you eat, to maintain a high level of discipline, to follow though on all things with diligence...*and* to practice your priorities!

What's a woman to do?! We'll find out the how-to's and practicalities for mastering these everyday challenges in this book about *God's Wisdom for a Woman's Life.* As we work our way through God's timeless principles for our every need, you'll discover...

- ways to improve your life one day at a time,

- insights for setting new priorities,

- a blueprint for a better life,

- small changes that bring order to your life, and

- tools for building the life you desire, a life marked by wisdom.

This is just a sample of the wonders you'll encounter on the journey we are preparing to take in this book—a journey to gain a practical working knowledge of the wisdom found in the Bible. Along the way we'll also gather timeless principles out of the book of Proverbs, the wisdom book of the Bible. As you can tell, we'll be looking in one place...and one place only for wisdom for your life as a woman—the Bible, for...

> "the LORD gives wisdom; from *His* mouth comes knowledge and understanding" (Proverbs 2:6).

A wise woman is a woman who is continually growing in wisdom. So don't miss out on the companion volume to this book, *God's Wisdom for a Woman's Life Growth and Study Guide.* Whether alone or in a group, you'll enjoy the additional scriptures and principles of wisdom in this study guide that address the day-in, day-out areas of your busy life.

Dear seeker of wisdom, wisdom is free. Wisdom is openly available. Wisdom is there for the taking. And furthermore, wisdom is actively seeking after you and me...if we would only respond to her call (Proverbs 1:20-23). So please join me in a life-changing journey toward creating a life of wisdom. Join me as we discover together God's wisdom for our every need.

God's Wisdom for...
Your Life

Wisdom is skill in living.[1]
Wisdom is the right use of knowledge.[2]
Wisdom is knowing what to do.
Wisdom is the ability to see with discernment.
Wisdom is the ability to view life as God perceives it.[3]
Wisdom is the God-given ability to see life
with rare objectivity and to handle life
with rare stability.[4]

I Need Help with...
*W*isdom

I don't know about you, but it seems like I have to make at least one decision a second! Sometimes I feel like life's demands are bombarding me on all fronts. And every assault calls for something from me—a word, an answer, a judgment call, an action, a choice. I have to decide what to think or not think, say or not say, ask or let lie, work on or wait on. I even have to determine whether to buy or not buy, pause or move into action, get up or sit down. In a word, what I need with my every breath is *wisdom!*

So...how does one get wisdom? After examining how one Old Testament man acquired wisdom, we'll set out the steps we can take to follow his example.

The Wisdom of Solomon

Long, long ago, about 3,000 years ago, Israel had a newly crowned king named Solomon. Solomon was the son of the mighty King David. He was new at being a king, he was somewhat young (1 Kings 3:7), he had lived his whole life in his father's shadow, and he was definitely inexperienced. As he quaked in his sandals and staggered under the weight of his new responsibility, Solomon did what you and I must learn to do. He took the first step toward wisdom. He humbled himself before God in prayer and *asked* for wisdom.

I'm sure you've heard the fairy-tale scenario "Ask anything you wish and it will be granted." Well, this is essentially what happened to Solomon. In a dream the Lord appeared to Solomon and said, "Ask! What shall I give you?" (1 Kings 3:5).

(What would you ask for, dear reader?)

Solomon shows us the right thing to ask for. He answered, "Give to Your servant an understanding heart to judge Your people, that I may discern between good and evil. For who is able to judge this great people of Yours?" (verse 9).

And the result?

Solomon's asking for wisdom and discernment pleased the Lord. Therefore God said to Solomon, "Because you have asked this thing, and have *not* asked long life for yourself, nor have asked riches for yourself, nor have asked the life of your enemies, but have asked for yourself understanding to discern justice, behold, I have done according to your words; see, I have given you a wise and understanding heart, so that there has not been anyone like you before you, nor shall any like you arise after you."

And then came the bonus!

"And I have also given you what you have not asked; both riches and honor, so that there shall not be anyone like you among the kings all your days" (3:11-13).

And by the way, Solomon became the wisest man who ever lived (other than Jesus Christ, of course). He is heralded as a man who spoke 3,000 proverbs (1 Kings 4:32). In the book of Proverbs you and I can read the best of his 3,000 proverbs. He was truly brilliant. Why? Because God blessed him and "God gave Solomon wisdom and exceedingly great understanding" (1 Kings 4:29).

Steps Toward Wisdom

What woman doesn't want to be, and be known as, a woman of wisdom? (And what woman doesn't need wisdom!) I know I do, and I believe you do too. As we look through Proverbs we discern these unchanging steps that will cause us to be women of greater wisdom.

Step 1—We must desire wisdom. Let's go a step further and say we must desire wisdom above all else. This is the step—the first step toward wisdom—that Solomon shows us. He desired wisdom. And he desired it above all the other things that the human heart can desire.

How do the desires of your heart measure up? Do you desire long life, riches, and triumph over your enemies (1 Kings 3:11), or do you desire wisdom? Check your heart. As Solomon teaches us, "Happy is the man [or woman] who finds wisdom, and the man who gains understanding; for her proceeds are *better than* the profits of silver, and her gain than fine gold" (Proverbs 3:13-14).

Step 2—We must pray for wisdom. Again, Solomon shows us the way to wisdom. He prayed for it! He recognized his need for wisdom…and he asked God for it. He didn't pray for a good marriage, for obedient children, or for money to pay the bills. No, he prayed, "Give me wisdom and knowledge" (2 Chronicles 1:10).

Dear friend, when you and I learn to pray for wisdom and knowledge, then we will have what it takes to have good marriages, obedient children, and money to pay the bills! It's all bound up in wisdom! What is it that you pray for? It's not wrong to pray for your marriage, family, and finances. But be sure you are primarily praying for the *one* thing that will help *every* thing in your life. Check your prayers. One of my favorite scriptures regarding wisdom (written by…who else but Solomon!) exhorts you and me to "cry out for discernment, and lift up your voice for understanding" (Proverbs 2:3). Echoing this wisdom about a thousand years later, James wrote, "If any of you lacks wisdom, let him ask of God…and it will be given to him" (James 1:5). So ask, precious one! Just ask!

Step 3—We must seek wisdom. The very next verses of Proverbs 2 teach us this vital step: "If you seek her as silver, and search for her as for hidden treasures; *then* you will understand the fear of the Lord, and find the knowledge of God" (Proverbs 2:4-5). In the initial days of studying my way through the book of Proverbs, I remember being impressed by the effort it takes a miner to excavate jewels, silver, and gold. It requires the proverbial blood, sweat, and tears! Why? Because such treasure does not lie exposed to the casual passerby. No one on a little stroll through life (or the Christian life!) will observe such riches by chance. No! They are buried. They are out of sight…sealed away, awaiting discovery. And only the diligent, the devoted, and the determined will put forth the strenuous labor required to find them.

Continuing along in Proverbs 2, a key passage regarding wisdom, Solomon tells us point-blank where to seek for wisdom. He explains, "For the Lord gives wisdom; from His mouth come knowledge and understanding" (verse 6). Here's our biggest clue yet to finding hard-won wisdom—it's in the Bible!

How diligently and strenuously are you seeking for the treasure of wisdom? Are you digging through the Bible? Are you searching the Scriptures daily (Acts 17:11)? Do your personal goals match up with this assignment from God to seek wisdom?

Step 4—We must grow in wisdom. Solomon has definitely provided us with a strong example of a person who desired wisdom, prayed for wisdom, and sought wisdom. But, unfortunately, he provides us with a negative example of a person who failed in this vital fourth step to wisdom—he did not grow in wisdom. Early in his life Solomon recognized his need for wisdom, sought it, and stunned the nation with his keen wisdom (1 Kings 3:16-28). But then he took many foreign wives who led him into idolatry, and his desire for wisdom and his follow-through on God's timeless principles of wisdom waned. In the end Solomon failed to obey God, neglected to grow in wisdom, and silently slipped off the pages of Scripture. Little is recorded about the last decade of Solomon's reign over God's people. Sadly, to this day, he is known not only for the wisdom God gave him, but also as the man who had "700 wives and 300 concubines" (1 Kings 11:3). What an epitaph!

I know we've looked at wisdom primarily through the life of Solomon, but now I want you to meet a woman who shows us the beauty (and benefits!) of godly wisdom. In contrast to King Solomon, she was not in a leadership position and did not have a prestigious title. No, she was a wife and a home manager, a woman very much like you and me. But...she was also a woman who just happened to possess a great measure of wisdom.

Meet Abigail

Abigail was a woman who had to make a decision-a-second, too. Married to an alcoholic tyrant named Nabal (meaning "fool"), you can only imagine the tightrope she walked. Yet Abigail is applauded as a woman of wisdom, a woman whose life was characterized by sound, wise actions and speech. Her most dazzling act of wisdom was averting a blood-bath between her foolish husband and the avenging warrior David and his 400 troops (1 Samuel 25). Abigail knew when to act...and did. She knew what to do...and did it. She knew what to say...and said it. What were some of the marks of dear Abigail's wisdom?

> She perceived the big picture.
>
> She kept her composure.
>
> She formed a plan.
>
> She spoke with wisdom.
>
> She effectively influenced others.

Abigail's life teaches us that every challenge or responsibility that lies before us can be handled in a godly way when we handle it with godly wisdom.

Just for Today...

Well, what will it be? Do you desire a life distinguished by wisdom...or the opposite, one marked and marred by foolishness? I think I know the answer. So let's see what we can do just for today to begin forming daily habits that will help us become God's women of wisdom.

❏ Just for today...read the chapter of the book of Proverbs that corresponds with the date of this month. Pick the one verse that most spoke to your heart and your life. Go a step further and write it on a 3" x 5" card. Carry it with you all day. Prop it up near the kitchen sink when you're at work in the kitchen. Lay it on the counter when you wash your face, brush your teeth, put on makeup, and fix your hair. Slip it into your purse to pull out and review when waiting at a red light. Have a goal to make the wisdom of that one proverb yours. Also ask yourself, Do I consider God's wisdom to be more valuable than silver and gold?

❏ Just for tomorrow…follow the exercise above. In fact, follow it for life. Seek the treasure of God's wisdom by reading just one chapter every day until you meet Him face to face. Imagine the wisdom you will possess! It's true that great things are gained by the smallest of efforts made just one day at a time. In addition, think about some decision you must make or some problem you are facing. Then heed the wisdom of Proverbs 15:22, which teaches us that "without counsel, plans go awry, but in the multitude of counselors they are established." Who will you ask for help?

❏ Just for this week…purchase or check out from your church library a commentary (a book of explanation written by a Bible scholar) on the book of Proverbs. Then, each day as you read, allow the wisdom and study of the scholarly author to enlighten your understanding of God's wisdom. This is one simple way to seek and search for wisdom.

Seeking a Heart of Wisdom

Throughout this book about *God's Wisdom for a Woman's Life* we will be searching for wisdom for our every need. We will be looking at what the Bible—the Book of Wisdom—has to say on a variety of life topics and issues that you and I face as women. We will also be surveying the small but practical book of Proverbs in the Bible—the wisdom book of the Bible.

However, after you have finished this book, you will need to continue your search for wisdom. Why? Because, other than Jesus Christ, the Son of God and God-in-the-flesh, no one has ever been born with wisdom. All must desire it, pray for it, seek it, and grow in it. I hope you will be growing in wisdom until the day you die.

So where can you begin right this minute? Open your heart now and hear these wise words of another: "The man who is truly wise is the man who finds out that he is a fool without Christ [Romans 1:22].... As long as a man rejects Christ, he is a fool. The wisest man is he who, in complete abandonment to self, bows before the Lord."[5]

Have you yet bowed yourself before the Lord?

More Wisdom Regarding...
Wisdom

The fear of the LORD is the beginning of wisdom,
and the knowledge of the Holy One is understanding.
Proverbs 9:10

Buy the truth, and do not sell it, also wisdom and instruction
and understanding.
Proverbs 23:23

Teach us to number our days,
that we may gain a heart of wisdom.
Psalm 90:12

I...do not cease to...[make] mention of you in my prayers:
that the God of our Lord Jesus Christ, the Father of glory,
may give to you the spirit of wisdom
and revelation in the knowledge of Him.
Ephesians 1:15-17

If any of you lacks wisdom, let him ask of God,
who gives to all liberally and without reproach,
and it will be given to him.
James 1:5

*H*ave two goals:
wisdom—that is, knowing and doing right—
and common sense. Don't let them slip away,
for they fill you with living energy and
bring you honor and respect.
Proverbs 3:21-22[1]

*P*ut first things first
and we get second things thrown in:
Put second things first
and we lose both first and second things.[2]

*T*he more you seek a heart of wisdom by
focusing on God's priorities for you,
and practicing those priorities,
the more you will eventually live by them.
Then yours will be a life marked by God's wisdom.
—*Elizabeth George*

2

I Need Help with...

My Priorities

One picture is worth a thousand words! And the picture God painted in Proverbs 31:10-31 of the wise woman *par excellence* has served me as a model of a woman who lived out her priorities. I'm so thankful that I found her in the Bible some 30 years ago. Through her portrait, you and I, as have women down through the centuries, can walk beside a "living" mentor through the span of her busy-but-orderly life. In fact, to this day whenever I read the 22 verses that depict the details of her daily life, I gain three things—renewed strength for my efforts, a fresh reminder of God's priorities for my life, and a new dedication to His plan for my time here on earth. Visiting with this lady is such an energy charge that I've memorized these scriptures so that I can carry her timeless wisdom with me in my heart. Then I can call upon her counsel at any time, in any place, and in every situation.

However, we women often look at the remarkable life of this woman from the Bible and marvel, "How did she do it all? This woman seemed to be *every*where at all times, taking care of *every*one and *every*thing! What was her secret?"

Thank the Lord the Proverbs 31 woman was no Wonder Woman or super hero! No, she was a woman just like you and me. But her distinctive mark was that she was a woman who knew her priorities *and* practiced them. And that, my friend, is a mark of wisdom. Many women don't know their priorities and therefore rush off in all directions at once or in no direction at all. Other women know their priorities but don't practice them, and end up walking through life with guilt and frustration. But the wise woman does both. Now, *that's* what we want! So...

What can we learn from this learned lady—and from other wisdom taught in the Bible—about the priorities of a wise woman? Exactly where should we be placing the emphasis of our time, our energy, and our devotion? Let's look to the Source for our answers.

Put God First

Top priority goes to God, who gets us started in the right direction. Our love for God and our devotion to Him are to be complete and all-consuming. The Proverbs 31 woman was praised and exalted by God and others. Why? Because she was "a woman who fear[ed] the LORD" (Proverbs 31:30). And, according to Proverbs 9:10, "the fear of the LORD is the beginning of wisdom, and the knowledge of the Holy One is understanding." Our Lord Jesus Christ put it this way, "'You shall love the LORD your God with all your heart, with all your soul, with all your mind, and with all your strength.' This is the *first* commandment" (Mark 12:30).

Exactly what does it mean to make God the reigning priority of our lives? To me it includes making one very practical decision every day—to read something out of God's Word. God is the source of all wisdom. He possesses all the wisdom there is. And He has revealed it in His Word, the Bible. As the psalmist put it, the law of the Lord makes the simple person wise (Psalm

19:7). So discovering God's wisdom by reading the Bible is a must for you and me as we seek hearts of wisdom.

And just to secure the place of this leading priority, I try to make—and follow through on—my decision to read the Bible early in the day. Better than that, I purpose to do it first thing each day. That's called putting first things first. My thinking goes like this: *I want God to be first in my life, so I'm putting Him first in my life today.* When you and I make (and don't forget the follow-through!) this one decision, we experience this truth: "Put first things first and we get second things thrown in: Put second things first and we lose both first and second things."[3]

If you want to follow in the steps of God's wisdom, do this one thing—before the day gets going (or gets out of hand!) and before the others in your household get going, curl up in some cozy place and read your Bible. Fill your mind with God's mind. This one simple act of beginning each day with God sets each day on the path of wisdom.

Serve Others

After Jesus made the statement in Mark 12:30 regarding the love you and I should have for God—a love that includes our obedience to Him—He next said, "And the *second* [commandment], like it, is this: 'You shall love your neighbor as yourself'" (Mark 12:31).

God first, others second. This is the order of priorities we witness lived out in the Proverbs 31 woman. The others in her life were her husband, her children, her helpers and co-workers, and those in her community. And these people received the overflow of her love for the Lord. Each day, after looking first to God and receiving from Him, this noble woman next turned her eyes, hands, and heart of love toward others. God's love was then extended to her family members and those priority people nearest to her. This lady's life was spent serving others. That's why she was praised by God, by her husband and children, and by the community. Why, even "her own works," her very accomplishments, "praised" her (Proverbs 31:28-31)!

Knowing God's order of priorities—God first and others second—helps me to plan each and every day. Understanding that I am to do all things *in* Him and *through* Him and *for* Him and *unto* Him gives my every day and every act of my every day an upward focus. Daily, I plan exactly how to bless and serve my husband, my two daughters and their husbands, and my five grandchildren. My planning extends to include my friends and neighbors, my church family, and the women I minister to. "God first and others second" is a simple way of living out God's will and wisdom for my life. And then the outpouring of service begins!

Planning to practice God's priorities—Why not take your planner in hand? Look at your plan for tomorrow. Does it include that priority time with God? If not, take pen in hand and mark it indelibly on your schedule as the first thing. When I consider this Number One act, I never fail to hear the echo of Jesus' words in my heart—"Without Me you can do nothing" (John 15:5).

Now that you've planned in first things first, look to see if the rest of tomorrow's plan includes your loved ones. First, list them. Now, *what* will you do for each one of them? And *when*? Make the appropriate markings. Then fill up the rest of the day with the multitude of activities that fill the rich, wonderful, multifaceted days of your life. And speaking of rich, what a rich reward you will receive at the end of a day spent in this way! Oh, you'll be tired. Count on it. But welcome it too. You'll be fulfilled because you walked in wisdom for just one day. You lived just one day according to God's top two priorities—God first and others second.

Let's review—I want to say just a word here about the two priorities we've already focused on—God and others—before I go on to address the area of *self*. It's important to realize the magnitude of God being first *before* all others. But I don't want you to miss another emphasis this order places on our daily life.

Eliminating nonessential activities. It's not only God *before* all others, but it's also *others* before a multitude of *other things* we could spend our time on. These other things can keep a woman from serving others, whether her husband, children, and parents or friends, neighbors, workmates, and people at church and in the community.

What kinds of other things? Things like laziness, too much sleeping in, napping, and lounging. Things like too much shopping and running around. Things like too much time spent on the telephone, on the Internet, watching TV, or working on hobbies...even things like too much time working at a job. It's easy to let attention to self (or should I call it selfishness?) crowd out our responsibility to take care of the first two priority areas of our lives—God first and others second.

Take Care of Yourself

Now, for yourself. Yes, there is a place for wisely taking care of yourself. We'll address more on this priority area in other sections, but I want to emphasize here and now that taking care of yourself aids you in serving God and others.

For instance, take these all-too-common scenarios (maybe even from your life!). You fail to exercise...so your back goes out or you find yourself trying to function in a depressed, defeated, discouraged, and lifeless state. You fail to watch what you eat...so you lack energy or develop high blood pressure. You fail to get your necessary sleep (there's that TV, Internet, and hobby time again!)...so you can't get up, get going, or get it together the next day. You fail to practice discipline in the pills you take or the caffeine you ingest…so you are unpredictable, unreliable, and unstable, causing the others in your life (not to mention the quality of your life!) to suffer. You fail to take your vitamin supplements or prescribed medications and to drink enough water…so you lack the vitality and health needed in your daily life of service to God and others.

I trust you are getting the picture. There is a danger in neglecting your health and good habits. After all, just where does the physical energy come from for living out God's priorities and roles for your life? It comes from taking care of yourself, another mark of wisdom.

And I hope you understand the distinction between selfishness and taking care of yourself. Selfishness is self-indulgence, self-serving, and self-focus, which hinders our service to God and others. Tending to yourself, however, enhances and strengthens your service to God and others. In other words, you take care of yourself *so that* you can live out God's priorities. As with all God's priorities, this one requires planning too.

So…get out that day planner again! You've already scheduled in #1–Time with God, and #2–Time for serving others. Now plan in #3–Time for taking care of yourself. For instance, *when* will you get up and go to bed? *When* will you eat…and *what*? *When* will you exercise…and *what* exercises? And don't forget your vitamin supplements—*when* will you take them? Your planning and your planner will help you to live out God's priority of caring for yourself.

When it comes to your*self*, follow this handful of God's timeless principles—

- ❧ deny yourself of overindulgence (Proverbs 23:2 and 30:8),

- ❧ examine yourself for any sinful habits (1 Corinthians 11:28),

❧ exercise yourself to godliness (1 Timothy 4:7), and

❧ develop self-control (Galatians 5:23).

Just for Today…

How do you and I become women of wisdom? One day at a time. By practicing God's timeless principles of wisdom one day at a time you and I cultivate a life marked by wisdom. So, let the application of what you've learned about God's priorities for your life begin today…and extend for a lifetime!

❑ Just for today…plan tomorrow according to the three priority areas of God, others, and self. Regarding your time in God's Word, what book of the Bible would you like to read or learn more about? If you don't know where to start, begin with Proverbs 31:10-31. Then regarding others, what will you specifically do for your husband, children, family members, friends (and the rest of the people in your life) to serve them? And for yourself, what's wrong and needs correction, or what's not what it should be and needs improvement? Take a long, hard look. Then plan to make changes tomorrow, for just one day.

❑ Just for tomorrow…follow your priority plan. Stick to your guns! And be prepared—you'll have to say *no*…to yourself, to your flesh, to your excuses. But, with God's help, you can do it. All you have to do is make it through *one day!* Get up when you planned to get up, read your Bible when you planned to read your Bible. Do the acts of love you planned that will signal to others that they are truly a priority. And take care of (or should I say, ride roughshod over?) yourself…for just one day. Wow, what a day that will be! And what a giant commendable first step toward applying God's wisdom!

❑ Just for this week…do the same each day. Seek to multiply your one good day by seven. And don't fail to record your progress. Journal your practical application of wisdom in this everyday discipline of priorities. Notice and note the strength (and wisdom!) you are gaining as you read your Bible. Then enter your list of good deeds performed for the people in your life. And please take time to log God's grace and your personal progress as you seek to master your own life. The act of taking time to keep a record will encourage you and bring glory to God as you seek a heart of wisdom and distinguish yourself as a woman of wisdom—a woman who knows…and practices…her priorities. Wow, what a week that will be! I know it will be a week you want to repeat…for life!

Seeking a Heart of Wisdom

I hope you noticed the proverb at the beginning of this chapter (Proverbs 3:21-22). One loud message the passage shouts to every woman who seeks a heart of wisdom is that wisdom can easily slip away. You can lose wisdom by failing to desire it, to grow in it, and to apply it. It is the constant exercise of wisdom that ingrains it into your life. And that makes all the difference in achieving your purpose of living a life of wisdom.

And the same is true of priorities. The more you seek a heart of wisdom by focusing on God's priorities for you and practice those priorities, the more you will eventually live by them. Then yours will be a life marked by God's wisdom.

More Wisdom Regarding...
My Priorities

A woman who fears the LORD,
she shall be praised.
Proverbs 31:30

The heart of her husband safely trusts her...
She does him good and not evil
all the days of her life.
Proverbs 31:11-12

She also rises while it is yet night,
and provides food for her household
and a portion to her maidservants.
Proverbs 31:15

She extends her hand to the poor,
yes, she reaches out her hands to the needy.
Proverbs 31:20

She...does not eat the bread of idleness.
Proverbs 31:27

Seek first the kingdom of God and His righteousness,
and all these things shall be added to you.
Matthew 6:33

God has purposes for our lives
which He has not yet revealed.
Therefore each day grows sacred
in wondering expectation.
—*Phillips Brooks*

With the gift of a whole, entire,
precious, and priceless day before you, ask:
"Lord how do *You* want me to live this day?
What is it that *You* want me to do with this one day
that You have given me?
What is the work You want me to accomplish today?"
—*Elizabeth George*

3

I Need Help with...
My Purpose

s I interact with women almost every day, whether through letters, the Internet, radio phone-ins, or in live question-and-answer sessions, I so enjoy hearing their hearts as they seek help with the different areas of their busy lives. "Help...I have four little ones!" "Help...I have grandchildren on one end of my busy life and failing parents on the other!" "Help...my husband is so busy trying to provide for the family that I feel like I never see him!" (And, believe me, I have my own personal set of "Help..." please!)

But what I mostly hear is that busy women tend to bog down in the day-to-day matters of their lives and fail to understand how the work they are doing today fits into God's purpose for their lives and their futures. We all forget to look beyond the moment with its urgency. We fail to look upward and forward, which can answer the great *why* and clarify the purpose for what we are doing, need to be doing, or are struggling with doing. Instead we muddle through each day, barely making it to its unglorious end, never comprehending its purpose and where it fits in the grand scheme of our life. Sadly, most women are merely eking out the hours of their one-day-at-a-time. Many, too, are muttering their way through that one-day-at-a-time, frustrated, hopeless, even bitter.

But here's a truth that sheds new light on each one-day-at-a-time—you and I have no guarantee on the length of our lives. No, all we have is our one-day-at-a-time. Therefore we must seek to live our one-day-at-a-time with the future and a purpose in mind. A clear understanding of God's purposes and a long-range view of life puts the mark of wisdom on our every day and its endeavors.

So I'm advocating that you constantly evaluate your answers to questions like…

> What is God's plan and purpose for my life?
>
> In the end, what do I want to have accomplished with my life?
>
> And how do I want my life to have contributed to others?
>
> What do I want to leave behind?

Let's take a quick look at some of the more important facets of a woman's life, facets that reveal the *whys* of life and its purpose. As we do, keep in mind that *purpose* is the object for which something exists or is done. For us that is God. *Purpose* is also the end in view, our future. Again, for us that is God. I'll be using words like *purpose, purposes,* and *future* interchangeably because not only is our purpose wrapped up in God, but our future is too.

Eternal Life

Our time on earth has its joys, but it also has its trials and sorrows. But no matter how hard or tiring our work on earth becomes, it is invigorating when we realize that at life's end we will enjoy the presence of the Lord forever. The anticipation of eternal life adds hope to each and every day and deed. If you're like me, you can endure almost anything if you know some reward is coming. And one reason why you and I can stand anything that comes our way is because of what we are able to look forward to—the magnificent inheritance of eternal life with God (1 Peter 1:3-4). We are assured that in God's presence there is "fullness of joy," and at His right hand await "pleasures forevermore" (Psalm 16:11).

Do you possess the hope of eternal life, my friend? It is a gift of God, you know, given to us through faith in His Son, Jesus Christ (John 1:12). If you do, you can live each and every day, no matter how difficult or dreary, in the sunshine of God's promise of eternal life. That's the best *why* of your life!

Spiritual Life

Having God's promise of eternal life, we must then nurture our spiritual lives. We were created *by* God and *for* God. Therefore, we should be growing spiritually each day, being conformed into the image of God's Son (Romans 8:29), renewing our minds (Romans 12:2) and our spiritual lives day by day (2 Corinthians 4:16).

God expects us to grow spiritually. In fact, a group of Christians in the Bible who failed to grow was chastised with these words: "By this time you ought to be teachers, [but] you need someone to teach you" (Hebrews 5:12). So, why grow? First and foremost, grow because God expects you to. It's one of His goals for your life. Therefore, it instantly becomes one of the purposes of your life.

But here's another reason—energy! One of the bright aspects of spiritual growth is the tremendous energy such growth brings to each day and each task. As we read the Bible, the supernatural power of the Word of God energizes every daily task. It brings God's perspective on our lives and on our work to each day and its duties. And that divine perspective then infuses us and our work with stamina, drive, purpose, enthusiasm...and energy! It's a case of the *why* (God's purposes) empowering and pushing and encouraging us into *what* we must do and have to do.

Practical Life

God's purposes are also revealed in the practical areas of our lives. For instance, what is your practical life made up of? If you're like most women, your list looks something like this:

Family life—If you are married, your daily life includes a husband. If you have children, add them to your practical-life list. Some have parents, brothers, sisters, and in-laws, too. The people God has placed in our lives become a part of His purposes for our lives. He means for us to invest our time, effort, energy, and money into our families. He even speaks in the Bible to our specific roles in each relationship. Therefore, doing what God says He wants us to do in these family relationships becomes a life purpose. If the only thing you and I ever leave behind with our lives or contributions to others is a godly imprint upon our families, then we will have lived out one of God's grandest purposes.

Physical life and health—Where does the physical energy come from for living out God's purposes and plans? From your body! And God has entrusted you with the stewardship of your body.

We all know that any neglect in our physical lives and health *will* ultimately bring consequences! Yet it's human nature to erroneously think that we have all the time in the world to fulfill God's purpose for ourselves in this area. You know—you're *going* to get around to it! You have great plans to change your eating habits, to exercise more, to take better care of yourself, to be more regular in taking your vitamin supplements, to reduce stress, to alter your lifestyle, to give up your bad habits...one of these days! And the whole time you're *meaning* to do something and *intending* to change, your bad habits and neglect are taking their toll...until one day it's too late, and your health is worse than you thought, jeopardizing the quality of your future.

How's your physical condition and your health? You can be sure that someday in the future what you're doing or neglecting to do in the care of your health will determine your quality of life. Now, what will that quality be?

Ministry life—Every day I ask myself the questions I shared earlier: In the end, what do I want to have accomplished with my life? And how do I want my life to have contributed to others? What do I want to leave behind? These are sobering questions about life, aren't they? Obviously caring for my family is an urgent priority and one of God's primary purposes. I must contribute to their lives positively and for Christ. But beyond them, in the end...how many lives will I have touched? People are one of God's purposes, for in the end, all God will redeem from this planet are the souls of people. So, how many women are you discipling, training, and teaching? How many people are you serving, helping, giving to, and talking to about Jesus Christ?

Daily Life

It's true that our days are numbered. Indeed, they are in God's hands. He and He alone knows the length of our days on earth. In reality, then, that makes the minutes of a day all we have. That means, as two age-old sayings go, "Today is all you have" and "There is no tomorrow"! Jesus taught these truths in His parable of the rich fool who tore down his barns to build bigger ones. What did God say to this man? "You fool! This night your soul will be required of you" (Luke 12:20).

No, the wise woman knows not to say or think or act as if "Today or tomorrow we will go to such and such a city" or do such and such a thing. Why? Because she knows the rest of the story: "You do not know what will happen tomorrow. For what is your life? It is even a vapor that appears for a little time and then vanishes away." She knows to say and think instead, "If the Lord wills, we shall live and do this or that" (James 4:13-15). She knows that today is all she has and there is no tomorrow!

Dear friend, each 24-hour portion that God chooses to give to you is to be lived *in* Him, *unto* Him, *for* Him, and *by* His strength. Why? Because today *is* the future! I repeat, today is all you have to live out God's purposes for your life. There is no guarantee of tomorrow.

The best thing about the future is that it comes only one day at a time. As the saying proclaimed, Today is all you have. That means today is the only future you have. Today is the only day you have to live out God's purposes. Therefore, how you manage today for God adds to the quality of the life—and future—you are building (and hopefully...and purposefully...building for His glory!).

Each day when I wake up, I can hardly believe how blessed I am. Just think, the gift of a day, a whole, entire, precious and priceless day! But (I remind myself)—it's not my day. Oh no. It's *God's* day! And I am a steward of it. So I sit down with my calendar and planner in hand and ask, "Lord, how do *You* want me to live this day? What is it that *You* want me to do with this one day that You have given me? What is the work *You* want me to accomplish today?"

This is how God's purposes are lived out in the present. Not a day is to be taken for granted. Not a day is to be wasted or frittered away. And every day is meant to count. What is it that makes a day count? Answer: Living it for God's purposes. So make it your purpose to focus on...

> ❧ A godly walk—"And what does the LORD require of you but to do justly, to love mercy, and to walk humbly with your God" (Micah 6:8).

❧ A passionate walk—The apostle Paul declared, *"Reaching forward to those things which are ahead, I press toward the goal for the prize of the upward call of God in Christ Jesus"* (Philippians 3:13-14). Catch the passion of such a purpose!

❧ A sober walk—Warning! God cries, "See then that you walk circumspectly, not as fools but as wise, redeeming the time, because the days are evil" (Ephesians 5:15-16).

❧ A wise walk—"Therefore do not be unwise, but understand what the will of the Lord is" (Ephesians 5:17). Make it your purpose to know and understand what God's will is as revealed through His Word.

Just for Today…

Knowing your purpose is a great motivating force. Make it a habit to each day reaffirm God's purposes for you and plan to live them out…just for today.

❏ Just for today…set your sights on God's purposes for your life. Pray, calendar and planner in hand, and ask, "Lord, how do *You* want me to live this day? What is it that *You* want me to do with this one day that You have given me? What is the work *You* want me to accomplish today?" Then live out those purposes in a godly, passionate, sober-minded, and wise way. Focus on *Him* and *them*, on God and on the people He has entrusted to you.

❏ Just for tomorrow…(if there is one!) welcome the gift of your new day, a whole, entire, precious, and priceless day! Then remember that it's not your day. It's *God's* day…and you are a steward of it. So take calendar and planner in hand and follow the path you took yesterday (see previous page).

❏ Just for this week…watch over your walk with God, watch over your family and loved ones, and watch over yourself. Focus on these purposes.

Seeking a Heart of Wisdom

I know this chapter is more "philosophical" than the others. But I put the subject of purpose here at the beginning of this book about God's wisdom for our lives for a reason. I know too many women (and I used to be one of them!) who cannot sustain the practice of the timeless principles God calls us to. These sweet women know the principles. And they want to apply them. But they simply cannot keep up with their good intentions.

Why would that be? Because they see no purpose in it. There's no reason to strive. There's no *why* for what they are doing or trying to do. My new friend, *purpose is the key to doing what we have to do to live our lives wisely.*

And what is it God is asking of us? What are His purposes for you and me? Beloved, God does not ask His women to do a thousand things, not even a hundred things. No, our all-wise God asks only a few things of us. In fact, I think what we've looked at here regarding God's purposes for us could be boiled down to just three—determine to obey God (1 Samuel 15:22). Develop a greater trust in the Lord (Proverbs 3:4-6). And devote your life to becoming more like Christ (Romans 8:29).

As we are faithful in these three areas, we will find and fulfill God's purpose in our lives. Any person, man or woman, who seeks to do these things will most definitely live a life of purpose (Ephesians 1:11; 2 Timothy 1:9).

More Wisdom Regarding...
My Purpose

LORD, make me to know my end,
and what is the measure of my days,
that I may know how frail I am.
Psalm 39:4

Trust in the LORD with all your heart,
and lean not on your own understanding;
in all your ways acknowledge Him,
and He shall direct your paths.
Proverbs 3:5-6

Wisdom is in the sight of him who has understanding,
but the eyes of a fool are on the ends of the earth.
Proverbs 17:24

Do you not know that those who run in a race all run,
but one receives the prize?
Run in such a way that you may obtain it.
1 Corinthians 9:24

Not that I have already attained, or am already perfected;
but I press on, that I may lay hold of that for which
Christ Jesus has also laid hold of me.
Philippians 3:12

God's Wisdom for...
Your Spiritual Life

*F*or the L<small>ORD</small> gives wisdom;
from His mouth come knowledge and understanding.
Proverbs 2:6

*G*od's Word is so exciting, so electric, so energizing—
in a word…thrilling.
But more than that, God's Word is life changing.
Its supernatural power is transforming,
and it provides pure wisdom!
For every need and issue and decision
that must be made in life, the Bible has the answers.
—*Elizabeth George*

4

I Need Help with...
My Bible

I don't know how passionately you feel about your Bible, but I can tell you that I consider my Bible to be my life! For the first 28 years of my life I looked in every direction (but up!) for help. I read the world's wisdom about how to have a better marriage. The same went for childraising. It's no wonder that, on both counts, things moved steadily from bad to worse. And my soul? I frantically sought peace in about every place and religion you can think of.

And then I was put in a situation where I was forced to read a "religious" book for a book review. The particular book I chose to review (because it was the only religious book in our house) quoted the Bible—*lots* of Bible. I mean, verse after verse of Bible! Soon I began suspiciously thinking, "The Bible doesn't say that!" At last I located my small white childhood confirmation Bible, dusted it off, and began to look up the Bible references. I was certainly unskilled at this (and maybe you can identify!). For instance, if the reference was Daniel 1:7, I turned to the table of contents in my musty-smelling Bible, looked up the page number to the book of "Daniel," then found the page and finally the verse.

And there they were! The scriptures quoted by the writer of my one-and-only religious book were right there in the Bible. And, as you and I both know, God's Word is powerful and mighty, and it went to work on my hapless heart and sinking soul. Before I finished reading that book, I became a Christian! I gave my life to Jesus Christ—every part and parcel of it. I was born again in Him and by Him and because of Him. I entered into His forever family, and thanks be to Him, my life has never been the same!

Since that day—the day I found out the truth about Jesus Christ in the Bible—I've been a helpless Bible addict. Even these 30 years later, I still can't take in enough of God's Word! In fact, my appetite for the life-giving, life-saving, problem-solving truths in God's Word has increased as the decades have paraded by. I have now passed through what are called...

The Three Stages of Bible Reading

Stage 1—The cod liver oil stage when you take it like medicine.

Stage 2—The shredded wheat stage when it's nourishing but dry.

Stage 3—The peaches and cream stage when it is consumed with passion and pleasure.[1]

Now for you, my reading friend. I want *you* to have this same delicious addiction, love, and passion for God's Word. I want it for you because God's Word is so exciting, so electric, so energizing—in a word...thrilling. But more than that, I want it for you because God's Word, your Bible, is life changing. Its supernatural power is transforming. And it provides pure wisdom! For every need and issue and decision that must be made in life, the Bible has the answers.

The Treasure of God's Word

At the beginning of this chapter I shared a verse from the book of Proverbs—"For the LORD gives wisdom; from His mouth come knowledge and understanding" (Proverbs 2:6). Therefore, Solomon, the writer of Proverbs 2, cries out to you and me regarding the gaining of wisdom, "*seek* her as silver, and *search* for her as for hidden treasures" (verse 4). Truly, the Word of God is treasure. Why?

The Bible comes from God—The Bible is "given by inspiration of God" (2 Timothy 3:16), every word of it. That means it is "God-breathed." There are no fads and no gimmicks in the Bible. What you read between the covers of your Bible is wisdom for a lifetime and rock-solid, forever truth, truth you can stand on, live by, and trust…forever!

I've already told you what the Bible, *God's* Word, means to me. Up until the day I dusted off that tiny Bible that had been given to a tiny girl (me!), I was lost in the pursuit of "the things of the world" (1 John 2:15). I read worldly books and listened to worldly voices. It was a baffling and frustrating life. Just when I was switching over my lifestyle to some particular view, along came another philosophy…and I had to start all over again. I had nothing to sink my teeth into, stand on, count on, or base my life on…until I found the Word of God. By contrast, God's truth will *never* change. *Never!* I repeat, in the Bible you and I have guidelines for our every need, for every issue, for every day, and forever.

That's my story. Now, what is yours? Where are you on the Floundering Scale? On the Seek-and-Search Scale? On the Bible Appreciation Scale? If you are struggling or drifting along in life,

I urge you to pick up a Bible and read away. If you need help in a relationship, with a problem, concerning a decision you must make, then set up a personal retreat where you can spend an entire day or weekend reading God's Word and praying. If you need a renewed passion for God's Word, then set aside time each day dedicated to reading some portion of the Bible. Immerse yourself in God's Word. And pray as you read. Commit yourself afresh to your spiritual growth, to your inner beauty, to the practice of reading your Bible. God's Word will make all the difference in the world…in every area of your life and for every need of your life.

The Bible causes you to grow in Christlikeness—A beautiful picture of the transforming power of God's Word is written in 2 Corinthians 3:18: "But we all, with unveiled face, beholding as in a mirror the glory of the Lord, are being transformed into the same image from glory to glory, just as by the Spirit of the Lord." With these words the apostle Paul was pointing out that all believers, as they continually focus on Christ, are transformed by the Holy Spirit more and more into His image.

I will never say that I am Christlike, but I will always say that I *desire* to be Christlike. And, as I read my Bible and pray, I gain wisdom for life from the Source of all wisdom. The simple exercise of reading your Bible is so rewarding and life-changing that you'll want to do it for life…which will add up to a lifetime of growing spiritually, growing in Christ, growing in the beauty of Christlikeness, *and* growing in wisdom.

And now, I ask you, what more do you and I need to convince us that a woman of wisdom is one who loves her Bible, who seeks knowledge and truth from God's Word? Like those who mine for silver and search for gold, you and I must *search* the Scriptures daily (Acts 17:11), diligently, doggedly, devotedly, and desperately! Our lives depend on it. As we mine the spiritual wealth of wisdom buried in the Bible, we then possess the treasure of the message of God to our hearts, a message that changes our hearts and transforms us into the likeness of our blessed Savior.

Beloved, my heart is brimming over at this very moment! I have three Bibles open on my writing desk right this second (with four more on the shelf to my left and I don't know how many—20? 30? 50?—more Bibles in Jim's library downstairs). And there's a chair in the corner of my office. I'm going to take a break now, grab my Bible, retreat to my easy chair, and pore over its pages yet again. Writing about the treasure of God's Word, reaching for the words to express its glory, and recalling the many wonderful changes it has effected in my life has created an urge I simply must respond to. I must go there now!

Unearthing the Treasure of God's Wisdom

(I'm back now.) Just how does our affection for God's Word grow? How does a book, made up of ink on paper and bound between two covers, translate into a passion, a passion that moves us to put out the effort required to gain the treasure? A few simple steps make it happen.

Step 1—Read it. I could add, *just* read it! Start anywhere. The only wrong way to read the Bible is *not* to read it. And don't make your Bible reading time an ordeal. Just get your cup of coffee, tea, or hot chocolate, sit down, open your Bible, and read. Or take it to the doctor's office, or the hair salon, or the beach or park, or on the airplane. Like a cup of nourishment, just sip away on God's Word, any and every place you are.

And while you're at it, read Proverbs. Expose yourself to God's wisdom every day by reading the chapter of Proverbs that corresponds with the date of the month. As I'm writing this sentence, it's November 24, which means I've revisited Proverbs 24 and its wise instruction about laziness (verses 30-34). (I always seem to need that reminder!)

Whenever I hear women share about a mistake or a bad decision they've made, I always wonder in my heart, "Dear sweet woman, haven't you read the book of Proverbs? If you had ever read the book of Proverbs, even *once*, you would know exactly what God says to do and not to do about that issue!" As I said, dear sweet reader, just read it!

Step 2—Study it. There are many methods and levels of Bible reading. But I can promise you that if you begin to read your Bible, it won't be long before you have a few questions. And that will lead you to studying the Bible.

That's precisely what happened to me as I began to read from the Proverbs every day. Soon I was wondering, "What in the world does *that* mean?" The same thing happened when I read about the women of the Bible. Growing up without Christian models, I turned to the women of the Bible for help. And soon the questions began to arrive.

So, I purchased my first commentary (a book of explanation written by a scholar) about the Proverbs. Then I sought out a book that specialized in the lives of the women of the Bible. And (you know the scene!) soon I was beginning to build a little library, one that also contains workbooks, study guides, and Bible studies of different books of the Bible. Begin small, dear heart, but do study your Bible.

Step 3—Hear it. We should never study God's Word in a vacuum. We need those who are gifted with knowledge and teaching ability to help us open the eyes and ears of our understanding. So be sure you regularly hear the Word of God expounded and explained (Hebrews 10:25).

Step 4—Memorize it. So many women tell me they can't memorize Scripture. Yet my three-year-old grandson Jacob is somehow able to memorize Bible verses. If a toddler can, you can! We don't always have a Bible in our hand, but we can have the Bible hidden away in our heart. Just make the commitment...and do it.

Step 5—Devour it. David wrote that God's Word was "sweeter...than honey and the honeycomb" (Psalm 19:10). Jeremiah testified, "Your words were found, and I ate them, and Your word was to me the joy and rejoicing of my heart" (Jeremiah 15:16). Job declared, "I have treasured the words of His mouth more than my necessary food" (Job 23:12). As you devour God's Word, you'll "taste" His refreshment too.

Just for Today...

How often do you eat? Daily! How often should you seek the Lord and His wisdom through His Word? Daily! Every discipline we are developing in this book is being tended to...one day at a time. So...

❑ Just for today...read your Bible! Doing so will stir your soul, encourage your heart, and fuel your faith. Don't miss out on God's wisdom today. And when you "discover" it, note it in your journal. Record the wisdom you find for your life. If you're not sure where to begin, begin with the chapter of Proverbs that corresponds with the date of the month. And here's a statistic—"By spending 10 minutes a day, you can read through the whole Bible in a year."[2] Couldn't you read 10 minutes...just for today?

❑ Just for tomorrow...continue what you began yesterday, but add Matthew, chapter 1. If you read one chapter in the Gospels (Matthew, Mark, Luke, and John) every day, you will read through the life of Christ once every three months. That's four times a year! Multiply that by the remaining number of years in your life, and...well, you will have a treasure house filled with the knowledge of your Savior's life. Then, whatever comes your way, you can (by His grace!) follow in His wise steps (1 Peter 2:21).

❏ Just for this week...think about another fact: Only about five percent of all Christians read through the Bible even once in their lives! By the time this week is over, you will be 1/52nd of the way toward joining the ranks of the elite "Top Five Percent"! If you are faithful just for this week, you will be well on your way to forging a habit that will reap eternal benefits. Peter put it this way: "All flesh is as grass, and all the glory of man as the flower of the grass. The grass withers, and its flower falls away, but the word of the LORD endures forever" (1 Peter 1:24-25). Be wise! Invest your time in something that lasts forever.

Seeking a Heart of Wisdom

Wow! Just think! It's all ours—God's inspired Word! And it causes us to grow in Christlikeness! And how does this powerful transformation take place? It's an inside job! *The Bible changes our hearts.* God's Word is alive and powerful, and it works on what's inside, on the heart (Hebrews 4:12). As you and I read the Bible, we learn God's truth, identify wrong behavior, mend our ways, and receive positive training in righteousness (2 Timothy 3:16). In other words, God's Word works us over from the inside out. It gives us a complete spiritual makeover and performs open-heart surgery at the same time. God's Word is God's ultimate beauty treatment for every woman.

This is certainly true for me. When I read my Bible, it penetrates my heart. It lifts my soul. It causes me to desire what God desires, to think more like God thinks, and to pursue what

God wants me to pursue. It changes my perspective on the people, events, and circumstances of my day and of my life. Then, when my reading time is over, I find my mind at rest, my heart at peace, my head clear, and a direction and purpose for my day—*God's* direction and purpose. May the same be true for you, dear heart-sister!

More Wisdom Regarding... My Bible

The statutes of the LORD are right, rejoicing the heart...
More to be desired are they than gold...
sweeter also than honey and the honeycomb.
Psalm 19:8,10

Your word I have hidden in my heart,
that I might not sin against You.
Psalm 119:11

Your word is a lamp to my feet and a light to my path.
Psalm 119:105

All Scripture is given by inspiration of God,
and is profitable for doctrine, for reproof,
for correction, for instruction in righteousness.
2 Timothy 3:16

For the word of God is living and powerful,
and sharper than any two-edged sword,
piercing even to the division of soul and spirit...
and is a discerner of the thoughts and intents of the heart.
Hebrews 4:12

*P*rayer does not fit us for the greater works;
prayer is the greater work.
Prayer is the miracle of redemption at work in us
which will produce the miracle of redemption
in the lives of others.
—*Oswald Chambers*

*S*tudy may make a biblical scholar;
but prayer puts the heart under heavenly teaching
and forms the wise and spiritual Christian.[1]
—*Charles Bridges*

I Need Help with
My Prayer Life

"Is that your cell phone ringing?"

We hear this every day, don't we? The technological era has certainly arrived in a big way in recent years. I remember getting my first cell phone. It seemed like it cost a fortune, and it was almost the size of my purse. Besides that, the air time was very expensive! So expensive, in fact, that to keep from receiving calls or being tempted to make a call, I would leave my precious cell phone off. Needless to say, that first cell phone wasn't much use.

My current cell phone, however, is far more useful—it's less expensive and more portable. So I'm not as hesitant to leave it on. In many ways my prayer life is like my current cell phone—I can pray anytime I want, anywhere I want, to anyone (God!) I want, for as long as I want.

But unlike my cell phone, there are no "roaming charges" when talking to God. I don't have to go to the time and trouble to scroll through my directory, select, and then dial a number. I don't even need to purchase any paraphernalia to enable me to talk "hands free" while I'm in the car. No, I have a direct channel to the God of the universe, twenty-four hours a day, seven days a week...to the Maker of heaven and earth. How's that for technology? *Divine* technology?

Developing a Prayer Life

With prayer being so easy, you would think that we would pray a lot more than we do. But prayer, like any other spiritual discipline, is just that—a discipline. And our natural man, our flesh and its sinful nature, resists any and all spiritual discipline. So you and I must make an effort to pray. Here are a few suggestions to help us develop our prayer lives.

Do it!—I could add, "Just do it!" Prayer, like any other habit, has to have a starting point. Why? Because we learn to pray by praying. Prayer is no different than learning how to cook, clean, care for a baby, type, paint, sew, use a computer, or the thousand others things you and I must do or are interested in doing. Experience is the best teacher.

Do it badly—When you first start learning to pray, you may think you are doing it badly. You may stumble and agonize over your words and concerns, but no prayer is ever done badly in God's eyes if your heart is right. Have you ever had one of your young children try to communicate with you? You appreciate their effort. You eagerly listen through the fidgeting and to the stuttering and jabbering as they search for words in their limited vocabulary. You hang on every sound so you can decipher their words and encourage them as they try. You don't want to miss a thing!

Well, precious one, your heavenly Father is like that too. And even more so because of His perfection. He is perfectly kind, perfectly patient, and He loves it when you and I come to

Him with our prayers, no matter how unpolished, simple, or childish.

Do it regularly—When I was in junior high school, I played the violin. I wasn't very good at it, even with practice. But for sure, you didn't want to hear me when I didn't practice! Prayer is like that. Prayer, like anything else done faithfully and regularly, in time becomes more natural and normal. But when we are irregular at prayer, we feel awkward and don't quite know what to say to God. God doesn't expect you to wait until you word your prayers flawlessly. He just wants to hear from you. Make it a habit to check in with God on a regular basis.

That's what David, "the sweet psalmist of Israel" (2 Samuel 23:1), did. He declared to God, "My voice You shall hear *in the morning*, O LORD; in the morning I will direct it to You, and I will look up" (Psalm 5:3). Another psalmist exulted, "*Seven times a day* I praise You" (Psalm 119:164), indicating that he prayed and praised numerous times because of a continual attitude of praise. When you fail to pray, you are in a sense saying you don't need God. (And here's another thought—when you fail to pray, you are also saying that you're probably not even *thinking* about God! How can I say that? Because any and every thought about God moves our hearts to pray.)

Do it faithfully—Faithfulness is a mark of maturity. A faithful person can be trusted in what they say and do. And faithfulness is a necessary element in any relationship, especially in a relationship with God. We all know that God is faithful. He is unchanging and unchangeable. Faithfulness is one of His attributes (James 1:17). So to keep up your part of a relationship with God, you need to be faithful to God. And the best way to be faithful is through a faithful prayer life.

And here's a side benefit to praying faithfully. Prayer helps you keep a clean slate with God. The Bible says if you and I are faithful to "confess our sins, He is faithful and just to forgive us our sins and to cleanse us from all unrighteousness" (1 John 1:9). Pray faithfully—it will keep you more faithful in your walk with God.

Do it for life—The breathing in of air sustains life. It's a basic fact—as long as we breathe, we live. Therefore no sane person would ever decide, "I think I'll take some time off from breathing." No, breathing is necessary for life. And you must see prayer in the same way. Prayer is necessary for the Christian life. Just as you will breathe for as long as you live, you must also pray for as long as you live. Do it for life.

Following a Model Prayer

Jesus was the wisest person who ever lived or will live. That makes Him the wisest teacher ever. And when it came to teaching others how to pray, Jesus wisely gave the disciples a model to follow. He didn't just say (as I've been doing) *Do it!*, *Do it badly*, *Do it regularly*, *Do it faithfully,* and *Do it for life.* No, the Master Teacher...*par excellence!*...gave His disciples a guide to follow. What is popularly called The Lord's Prayer has become a perfect pattern for prayer. A closer look at our Lord's model prayer gives us a better understanding of how to pray. Read these well-loved words now along with some insights into timeless principles on prayer drawn from them. Jesus, simply and straightforwardly, left no room for guesswork. He said to His followers, "When you pray, *say*..." (Luke 11:2), and...

> In this manner, therefore, pray:
> Our Father in heaven,
> hallowed be Your name.
> Your kingdom come.
> Your will be done
> on earth as it is in heaven.
> Give us this day our daily bread.

And forgive us our debts,
as we forgive our debtors.
And do not lead us into temptation,
but deliver us from the evil one.
For Yours is the kingdom
and the power
and the glory forever.
Amen (Matthew 6:9-13).

Prayer is personal. If you are one of God's children, you can talk to Him just like you talk to your physical father. And just as you would respect your earthly father, you are to be respectful of your Father in heaven. He is not "the Big Guy upstairs," "the Force," or "Mother Nature." Christ's model prayer begins with the very personal—and respectful—phrase, "Our Father in heaven."

Prayer acknowledges God's authority. The phrase "Your kingdom come" (verse 10) recognizes God's rule. His physical kingdom is now in heaven but will soon be here on earth. That means you are a kingdom child, waiting for the kingdom—and the King of kings!—to arrive.

Prayer acknowledges your trust. As a Christian, you do not accept such beliefs as fate, coincidence, luck, chance, or karma. That's because *nothing* in your life happens by accident. And nothing ever will. When you pray, "Your will be done" (verse 10), you are saying you trust a sovereign God to fulfill His perfect plan for your life.

Prayer indicates your dependence. You acknowledge that God is your sustainer and provider when you pray "Give us this day our daily bread" (verse 12). You must never forget that God supplies your needs, every one of them. Whether your realize it or not, you are absolutely dependent on His benevolence…even for the very "bread" you put in your mouth each day.

Prayer entreats God's guidance. "Life is a jungle!" is an often-quoted description of our existence on this earth. It's easy to get lost in a jungle...but not if you have a guide. Your omnipresent, ever-present Guide watches out for you: "Do not lead us into temptation, but deliver us from the evil one" (verse 13). On the positive side, God guides you "in the paths of righteousness" (Psalm 23:3).

Just for Today...

How do you and I become women of wisdom? I'm sure you've heard me say this a hundred times already, but here it is again, #101...one day at a time! And how do we cultivate a life marked by wisdom? Again, by practicing God's timeless principles of wisdom one day at a time. And, my friend, your prayer life is one of God's wisdom principles that absolutely must be practiced today, everyday, and for a lifetime! Martin Luther, the father of the Protestant Reformation, called prayer "the most important thing in my life." He admitted, "If I should neglect prayer for a single day, I should lose a great deal of the fire of faith."

Do you want wisdom for your life, for your complex, complicated, busy, spinning life? Then please, ask for it! God promises, "If any of you lacks wisdom, let him *ask* of God, who gives to all liberally and without reproach, *and it will be given to him*" (James 1:5).

❏ Just for today...make a decision to ingrain the habit of prayer deeply into your life. If you are not accustomed to praying, begin your prayer habit by setting aside just five minutes for prayer today. I even suggest using your kitchen timer. Then as we will learn in our chapter on scheduling, schedule your prayer time. Put it on your daily planner like you do all your other appointments. Next, make a list of things to talk to God about, to talk over with Him. Start with your family. Name them to God one by one, and share your concerns about them.

If you're already in the habit of praying, consider beefing up your commitment. What a privilege it is to pray for others, to be a "prayer warrior" on behalf of others, to literally pray around the world for God's people, to be "praying *always* with *all* prayer and supplication in the Spirit, being watchful to this end with *all* perseverence and supplication for *all* the saints" (Ephesians 6:18)!

❑ Just for tomorrow...set up some kind of system or notebook for keeping records of your prayer concerns. *Who* would you like to bring before your heavenly Father? *What* would you like to pray for them? *What* do you need to pray about personally? What character issues? What family problems? What are the areas where you need God's wisdom? Just make a list, write down the date you prayed, and lift your prayers before God's throne of grace (Hebrews 4:16). Be bold (Hebrews 4:16 again)! And don't forget to leave room on your prayer list for God's answers to your pleadings. Start small...and then watch for the mighty effect of your faithful prayers!

❑ Just for this week...continue to faithfully pray for those people and issues noted on your prayer list. When you've been regular for a week, increase the amount of time to a measure that indicates growth in this spiritual discipline. As you are faithful to pray and as you witness God's answers to your prayers, your faith will be strengthened and your commitment to prayer will grow even stronger. You will definitely want to repeat this wonderful week for life!

Seeking a Heart of Wisdom

Developing an effective prayer life isn't as intimidating as most people think. God doesn't care so much about how you pray as long as your heart is right (Proverbs 15:8). God, however, does want you to glorify Him by acknowledging His presence and your dependence on Him through prayer.

God also wants to bless you, His child, and grant your requests and all other "good things" (Matthew 7:11), but...He asks that you ask. "*Ask* and it will be given to you....For everyone who *asks* receives.... Your father who is in heaven give[s] good things to those who *ask* Him!" (Matthew 7:7-11). So, go ahead! Ask away! But take heed to this warning regarding your asking (and your heart!): "You do not have because you do not ask. You ask and do not receive, because you ask amiss, that you may spend it on your pleasures" (James 4:2-3). Don't be like the coed who disguised her selfish motive with this prayer: "Lord, I'm not asking for myself, but please send my mother a son-in-law!"

Dear heart, let's be serious about prayer. Let's join ranks with God's faithful corps of praying women—wives, mothers and mothers-in-law, daughters and daughters-in-law, grandmothers, aunts, and co-laborers. Let's remember that "the effective, fervent prayer of a righteous [woman, wife, mother, mother-in-law, daughter, daughter-in-law, grandmother, aunt, and co-worker] avails much" (James 5:16). If it's true that "prayer moves the hand of God," then we, my friend, have work to do—*serious* work! Let's follow the examples and prayer patterns of some of the Bible's heroes of prayer and ask for the right things. Read "The Power of Prayer" that follows. Take your time. Think about it. Let it inspire you...and change your prayer life forever!

The Power of Prayer

Moses prayed. His prayer did save
    a nation from death and from the grave.
Joshua prayed. The sun stood still,
    his enemies fell in vale and hill.
Hannah prayed. God gave her a son;
    a nation back to the Lord he won.
Solomon prayed, for wisdom he asked.
    God made him the wisest of men for the task.
Elijah prayed with great desire.
    God gave him rain, and sent the fire.
Elisha prayed with strong emotion;
    he got the mantle and a "double portion."
Jonah prayed. God heard his wail;
    He quickly delivered him from the whale.
Three Hebrews prayed, through flames they trod;
    they had as a comrade the "Son of God."
Daniel prayed. The lion's claws
    were held by the angel who locked their jaws.

Ten lepers prayed, to the priests were sent;
>Glory to God! They were healed as they went.
The thief who prayed—for mercy cried;
> he went with Christ to Paradise.
The disciples kept praying. The spirit came,
>with "cloven tongue" and revival flame!
Conviction filled the hearts of men;
>three thousand souls were "born again!"
The Church, she prayed, then got a shock
>when Peter answered her prayer with a knock!
Peter prayed, and Dorcas arose
>to life again, from death's repose.
When Christians pray, as they prayed of yore,
>with living faith, for souls implore,
In one accord, united stand—
>revival fires shall sweep the land!
And sinners shall converted be,
>and all the world God's glory see![2]

More Wisdom Regarding...
My Prayer Life

The eyes of the LORD are on the righteous, and
His ears are open to their cry....
The righteous cry out, and the LORD hears,
and delivers them out of all their troubles.
Psalm 34:15,17

Certainly God has heard me;
He has attended to the voice of my prayer.
Psalm 66:19

The sacrifice of the wicked is an abomination to the LORD,
but the prayer of the upright is His delight.
Proverbs 15:8

The LORD is far from the wicked,
but He hears the prayer of the righteous.
Proverbs 15:29

One who turns away his ear from hearing the law,
even his prayer shall be an abomination.
Proverbs 28:9

Little things come daily, hourly within our reach,
and they are not less calculated to set forward
our growth in holiness than are the greater occasions,
which occur but rarely.[1]

The greatest hindrance to our spiritual development
—indeed, the whole hindrance—
is that we allow our passions and desires to control us,
and we do not strive to walk
in the perfect way of the saints.
When we meet the least adversity,
we are too quickly dejected and
we turn to other people for comfort,
instead of to God.[2]
—*Thomas à Kempis*

6

I Need Help with...
My Spiritual Growth

ow blessed I am to have not just one but a corps(!) of godly mature women who have discipled and mentored me through my years as a Christian. Many dear female saints have left their fingerprints on my soul as they inspired, admonished, exhorted, and encouraged me, especially through those first few years of my spiritual development. As I began to grow and study the Bible on my own, I came across Titus 2:3-5. It was then that I began to realize that my corps of godly women were living out and modeling the qualities of the "older women" found in these verses.

Now, you might be thinking, *Who wants to be an old woman?* And you're right. No one wants to get old. But I'm not talking about physical age. I'm talking about spiritual age—maturity and wisdom, the qualities we are aiming at throughout this book. Like my "older women" who have had such an impact on my life, you and I should have as our goal to become true biblical "older women" ourselves. A dream-come-true for us would be to become women who have the maturity and wisdom to help our younger-in-the-Lord sisters. How do you and I become these mature, wise women who are available as models for others? The answer is…through spiritual growth.

Pursuing Spiritual Growth

To help us understand what it means to be growing spiritually, I've spelled it out. Spiritual growth is spelled…

W-I-S-D-O-M

W—*Willingly give your life to Jesus Christ.* Receiving Jesus as your Lord and Savior is the beginning of spiritual life. It is also the beginning of all spiritual growth. And it is the beginning of all wisdom. You cannot have growth without life. Nor can you have *spiritual* growth without *spiritual* life. Beloved, Jesus *is* the source of life (John 11:25)! Once you become a Christian, the Holy Spirit begins to work in your heart to fulfill God's will for your life. And God's will is that you grow spiritually (1 Peter 2:2 and 2 Peter 3:18).

I know I've asked this question before, but are you alive in Christ (Ephesians 2:5)? Wisdom begins in Him!

I—*Identify sin in your life.* I'm always so saddened when I see a child with some sort of growth defect. My heart and prayers always go out to the child and his parents, because our family has gone through just such an experience. Everyone knows that it's unnatural for something to hinder the normal growth process in a child's physical body. Thank God that He is able to cause all things—even a birth defect—to work together for good (Romans 8:28)! But just as something hinders a child's *physical* growth, sin for you and me is that "something" that hinders our *spiritual* growth.

What is sin? Sin is any thought, word, or deed that goes against God's standards presented to us in His Word, the Bible. Therefore, to grow spiritually, sin must be dealt with. We must be constantly identifying sin and purging it from our lives so that it doesn't hinder our growth as Christians. We are commanded to be "laying aside all malice, all guile, hypocrisy, envy, and all evil speaking…that you may grow" (1 Peter 2:1-2). This means to treat these sins like you would treat a dirty, filthy, soiled garment. Strip yourself of them!

Do you desire to grow spiritually? Then take a few minutes to reflect on the pattern of your life. Are there any glaring sin areas? Are there any flashing red lights of warning? Are there any blips on your growth screen? Are there any unconfessed sins? Any dirty garments? Quickly acknowledge them to God! Lay them aside! Be done with them! Deal with them…and deal with them ruthlessly. Please, don't let anything block or handicap your growth. Confess your sin…and then experience God's wonderful forgiveness and cleansing (1 John 1:9). "*Blessed* is he whose transgression is forgiven, whose sin is covered" (Psalm 32:1).

S—*Shed spiritual laziness.* It's frightening that I have so many choices to make each day when I get out of bed. For instance, I must choose to spend some time that day in physical exercise…or choose to let it slide for another 24 hours. (And this is only one of *many* choices I must make each and every day.) Another of those choices involves whether I will…or will not…spend some time in the study of God's Word.

Well, dear heart, since you and I want to grow spiritually and in wisdom, I'm advocating that we call our negligent choices exactly what they are—laziness! When you and I choose not to exercise, we are choosing to be physically lazy. And even more serious, when you and I choose not to be in God's Word, we are choosing to be spiritually lazy. That means we will not continue to grow in maturity. Why? Because our growth requires the strength and stimulus and nourishment that comes from God through His living, powerful, life-changing, growth-producing

Word. The remainder of 1 Peter 2:1-2 (see above) adds this truth about the Scriptures—and about our eagerness(!): "as newborn babes, *desire* the pure milk of the word, that you may *grow*" (verse 2). Why not honor God and make a renewed commitment to make some better choices about your use of time? Why not choose to make the best choice—to spend more time with God in His Word?

D—*Decide the method and rate of growth.* What's so wonderful about choosing to grow spiritually is that there are so many good tools available to help you grow. Depending on your lifestyle, responsibilities, and schedule, different types of study aids are available. You may want to start with resources that will help you study the Bible by yourself. You may want to get involved in a woman's Bible study at your church. Or you may want to consider these possibilities:

- Listen to the Bible on tape or to audiotapes of your favorite Bible teacher or preacher.

- Listen to cassettes or view videos of the teaching of God's Word by more mature women who can help you grow as a Christian woman.

- Read good Christian books on spiritual life and spiritual growth.

- Attend Bible-teaching seminars.

- Start memorizing key Scripture verses.

- Utilize a combination of these practices and then take the next step—find someone to disciple you.

If you are perhaps more mature in the Lord and just might be tempted to think, *Ho hum, I already know all this and do all these things,* then I have your next assignment. *Decide the rate of growth*. There's growth…and then there is growth! There is always room for more growth in our growth. So I'm suggesting that you up your rate of growth. However many minutes you read your Bible now, double it. Whatever you are studying, spend twice the time. Whatever you are memorizing, memorize more. Go a step further and do a study on the verses you are hiding in your heart. Instead of attending so many seminars, try teaching one! Instead of yawning at what we're learning (that you may already know), how about taking your incredible knowledge and passing it on to a younger woman in the faith? And here's another challenge—the same gentleman who gave the statistic of "it takes ten minutes a day to read through your Bible in a year" also gave this one: "By spending 15 minutes a day you can read 25 books in a year."[3] How many books have you read so far this year? Let's see some radical growth! Let's be radical! Let's be bold!

O—*Obligate yourself to be discipled.* As a new believer, I wanted to grow. Therefore I determined to be a learner. I knew I didn't know anything. In fact, I was beginning at about minus ten! So I went looking for someone who knew more than I. (And believe me, in my immature state, I didn't have to go very far to find someone!) I am eternally grateful to those who patiently worked with me and gently encouraged my spiritual growth. Some pushed. Some pulled. And some carried me part of the way. I often use the apostle Paul's words whenever I attempt to express my gratitude—"I am a debtor to" these loving saints (Romans 1:14).

Do you want to grow spiritually? I know you do. Then look for another woman who has the maturity and experience you need—that biblical "older woman," and ask for her help. If she's unable to help at this time, ask her to point you in the direction of someone who can help. Keep searching and don't give up! Unfortunately, "so far in the history of the world there have never been enough mature people in the right places."[4] Just maybe *your* growth will make a difference someday in the life of another woman!

M—*Maintain spiritual growth.* Spiritual growth must be a life-long pursuit. Growth in spiritual maturity is gained moment by moment, day by day, and year by year. In many ways, spiritual development is a lot like physical exercise. If you stop exercising, it might not show for a while. But one day you will wake up to find everything sagging in all the wrong places and that you've lost some physical strength.

In the same way, you deceive yourself into thinking that you can get along just fine without the Bible, prayer, and discipleship. One day, however, you wake up to a tragedy or a crisis and find you have very little spiritual strength with which to meet a personal emergency on that day. Don't put off growth. And don't be sporadic. Dedicate yourself to ongoing spiritual growth—for life. Maturing comes in the good times to prepare you for the bad times.

Just for Today...

Now, one more time—how do you and I become women of wisdom? And the answer, one more time—one day at a time. How do we cultivate a life of spiritual growth? By practicing God's timeless principles of wisdom...one day at a time. Spiritual growth comes in the daily exercise of spiritual disciplines— disciplines that become ingrained in your daily life—a habit that extends for life. So, one more time...

❏ Just for today...ask God to give you a desire for greater growth. Ask Him to reveal any hindrances to your spiritual growth. A hindrance could be sin, or it could be sinful people. Either will stifle your growth. Create a Bible-reading plan that fits into your schedule. Can you

think of a mature older woman who might disciple you?
Begin praying now about calling her.

❑ Just for tomorrow…continue on your reading plan. Be
faithful. Look forward to the growth it will generate.
Dream of growing in the grace and knowledge of your
Savior. And dream of passing on what you are learning
to help others—those in your own family, church, and
group of friends and associates. Continue to pray about
calling an "older woman" and asking for help. Go a step
further and begin a list of what you would want her to
teach you. Also, through prayer, identify areas of spiritual immaturity and laziness. Then ask God for help
from His Word or for wisdom in asking advice from a
mature woman. As God leads you, do something radical concerning your spiritual growth. What will that be?
Be bold!

❑ Just for this week…continue your Bible reading plan for
the week. By the end of your week, whisper a prayer to
God and call the "older woman" you've been praying
about contacting. At the end of the week ask God to
bring to your remembrance the truths you studied this
week. Continue on the next week and the next, for life.
Get excited. It's like exercise. When you exercise, you
think more clearly. You have more energy. Similarly,
when you exercise your spirit, you're more spiritually
alert, more discerning of the good and evil that come
your way. You begin gaining incredible strength and
building momentum as you build a life of wisdom.

Seeking a Heart of Wisdom

When I open my seminars on *A Woman After God's Own Heart*, I usually quote Psalm 33:11—"The counsel of the Lord stands forever, the plans of His heart to all generations." If you and I truly believed this verse, then we would understand why God's Word is so important.

What better *source* of wisdom is there than "the counsel of the Lord?" What better *confidence* can we have than knowing that God's wisdom, "the plans of His heart to all generations," is sufficient and enduring throughout every stage and age of our lives? And what better *legacy* can we leave behind than to pass on God's eternal wisdom to the next generation of women through discipleship?

Spiritual growth naturally leads to the wisdom you need for your life and the lives of those who come in contact with you. So seek a heart of wisdom! Grow spiritually, and you will be the source of great strength and hope for all those God brings across your path.

More Wisdom Regarding...
My Spiritual Growth

The righteous shall flourish like a palm tree,
he shall grow like a cedar in Lebanon.
Those who are planted in the house of the LORD
shall flourish in the courts of our God.
They shall still bear fruit in old age;
they shall be fresh and flourishing.
Psalm 92:12-14

He who gets wisdom loves his own soul;
he who keeps understanding will find good.
Proverbs 19:8

Those who wait on the LORD
shall renew their strength;
they shall mount up with wings like eagles,
they shall run and not be weary,
they shall walk and not faint.
Isaiah 40:31

As newborn babes,
desire the pure milk of the word,
that you may grow thereby.
1 Peter 2:2

Grow in the grace and knowledge
of our Lord and Savior Jesus Christ.
2 Peter 3:18

God's Wisdom for...
Your Daily Life

Take time to work—it is the price of success.
Take time to think—it is the source of power.
Take time to play—it is the secret of
perpetual youth.
Take time to read—it is the fountain of wisdom.
Take time to be friendly—it is a road to happiness.
Take time to dream—it is hitching your wagon
to a star.
Take time to love and be loved—it is
the privilege of redeemed people.
Take time to care for others—it is
too short a day to be selfish.
Take time to laugh—it is the music of the soul.
Take time for God—it is
life's only lasting investment.[1]

7

I Need Help with...
My Time

hen it comes to time and the lack of it, two time-management experts have this to say: "We so often hear, *I wish I knew how to manage my time better*. Rarely do we hear, *I wish I knew how to manage myself better.* To manage our lives we must then obviously learn to manage ourselves. Actually good time management is the only way we can possibly get more time for the things we *really* want to do."[2] And, I would add, the things we really *need* to do!

Where has the time gone?

I'm sure you've asked yourself this question on the many days when your dreams and good intentions have simply gone up in smoke. The day is over, you're exhausted, and you wonder, *Where has the time gone?*

Actually time didn't go anywhere. It's still here. It is still passing at the rate it always does...60 minutes in each hour... 1,440 minutes in each day...168 hours in each week. As we seek God's wisdom regarding our time, the better question we should be asking is, How could I have managed my life better in order to use the little time I do have?

I'll get to it when I find the time.

This is yet another statement that you and I are fond of making without thinking of its ramifications. Time isn't hiding from us, waiting to be found. No, time is right in front of us...right now...awaiting our beck and call...intended to be put to wise use. No, *time* isn't lost. We, however, are the ones who have lost the *use* of the time allotted to us when we fail to use it wisely.

So when you and I say, "I need help with my time," we are actually asking for help to manage our lives by using our time more wisely. We'll never be able to "manage" time itself, for time has some strange qualities. For instance...

Time cannot be bought or rented.

Time cannot be saved—you cannot store, freeze, or can time.

Time cannot be manufactured.

Time expands before your baby arrives and contracts after the delivery.

Time is slower for your children than for you.

Time is slower for you than for your dentist.

Time was slower for you as a student than for your teachers.

Time is slower for you in church than for your pastor.

As you can see, the issue is really life—not time. We need to understand how we can better manage our lives.

Managing Your Life

One timeless life-management principle is this—*learn to prioritize!* And to guide us in this process, God gives us as women some very specific job assignments and priorities in several passages in the Bible.[3] I have written at length about our priorities as women in the book *A Woman After God's Own Heart.*®4 But the point is, knowing your priorities is so very important. In fact, as has been stated, they are life determining! "Priorities are not just marginal options…. They are life determining. One's personality is molded inescapably into the image of his priorities."5 What a powerful statement about prioritizing your life! If you and I would simply focus our time, life, and attentions on these few areas that God has given us to manage, our time would be much more manageable. So take time for the following priority areas in your life.

Prioritizing Your Time

Time with God—I know I've said it before (and I'll probably say it again!), but God is to be your ultimate priority. Like Jesus said, when you "seek first the kingdom of God and His righteousness," all the other "things" in your life will fall into place (Matthew 6:33). Be sure you make Him your first priority each day. Give Him your early time before the family is up and the day—and your time!—is lost, squandered, and misused. Give Him your first time, the first fruits of each new and glorious God-given day.

Time with your husband—If you are married, after your time with God, your time with your husband is of next importance. Your husband is a gift from the Lord. Therefore thank God for him and take seriously your God-given assignment to love your husband…which takes time, and to serve your husband… which takes time. Take your cue from the Proverbs 31 wife— "she does him good and not evil *all the days of her life*" (verse 12). Now, that's *time!*

Time with your children—After God and your mate, your children are the next priority on God's list. Your time at home with your children during their growing-up years goes so quickly! Don't miss out on a single moment of this "season" and stewardship from God. (What if Hannah hadn't dedicated herself to her little Samuel during his early years at home?—1 Samuel 1:22-23) And don't stop giving time to your children after they leave the nest. Plan to spend time with them in their homes. And don't stop with your children. Your grandchildren need as much of your time as you can give them!

Time for family and friends—Absence does not make the heart grow fonder when it comes to family and friends. You have a responsibility from God to love and care for your parents, which again takes time. You also need to cultivate meaningful relationships with your siblings. You've gone through a lot together during the growing-up process. Now, don't lose contact with them. They are part of your heritage. They are part of your life and should be a part of your children's lives as well.

And don't forget your friends. They, too, need some of your time. But watch out—the problem with many women is that they short-change and neglect their husbands and families and focus their time on their friends instead. Your friends need your fellowship, but never at the expense of your family!

Time for yourself—Have you ever thought of your life as being like a battery needing to be recharged on a regular basis? Your life is also like a flower that unfolds with the passing of time. When you plan in some time for yourself to grow spiritually, to develop your spiritual gifts, to refine your talents, and to grow as a person, you are preparing yourself for a ministry to others. If you want to have an influence on others, plan time for yourself. Be sure you "*grow* in the grace and knowledge of our Lord and Savior Jesus Christ" (2 Peter 3:18).

Time for the unexpected—I confess here's where I fail regularly. I'm sure you've heard of Plan A and Plan B. Plan A is the plan you carefully and prayerfully make for your day...when you are sane and "things" are sane. In other words, if everything went without a hitch, your day would follow Plan A and become your perfect dream day come true! Plan B, though, is your backup plan. It's the plan you so often are forced to move to because of the unexpected, the unplanned, the surprises, or what I'm learning to accept as "the God-factor."

Here's what usually happens. You get up, you have your time with the Lord, and you make your sparkling Plan A. Then you move out on your Plan A day. Things are going well...until the telephone rings and you learn that someone is sick and needs a meal for that evening. Suddenly, whether you like it or not, and whether you planned for it or not, you've moved on to Plan B. And (and as I said, I'm learning this) that's OK! Because you have learned to view such Plan B scenarios as opportunities from the Lord for you to serve someone else, you have also learned to expect and cope with the unexpected. Therefore you quickly and quietly (without a fuss or a complaint) move to Plan B. Oh, to be like Jesus in this grace! He shows us perfectly the grace of handling interruptions (see Matthew 9:18-26).

Time for planning—How do you make time work for you, rather than becoming its slave? By planning. You must spend a short time daily thinking and praying about today and tomorrow, and even a longer period of time weekly thinking and praying about the week ahead. And then annually, try to make an opportunity to retreat and plan for the upcoming year. Planning will help you begin to manage your life and your priorities in a way that honors God and serves others.

Time for work—What I mean by *work* here is a job or occupation outside the home. I know you *work*. (What woman doesn't!) After all, you are a wife, mother, chef, gardener, handy woman, chauffeur, etc. You already have a full-time job with just the responsibilities at home! But if you also work outside the home, you *really* need to plan your day. Someone else is demanding eight hours of your day. So you must know how you are going to manage the other sixteen hours.

Learning What's Important

Learn to be more effective—The Bible shows us examples of women who were very effective. One such woman—the Proverbs 31 woman (Proverbs 31:10-31)—I've already mentioned in this book. When I read about her life, her time, and her wisdom, I have often asked myself, "How did this woman get it all done?!" Well, in a word, she got it all done because she was *effective*. Someone might say she was *efficient*. True, this woman did all her tasks well. That's what efficient means—doing tasks well. But more importantly, this woman did the *right* things well. That's effectiveness!

Now are you beginning to see why prioritizing your life is so important? You can do a lot of things in your busy, fast-paced life, and you can do them well. You can be extremely efficient, but...are they the right things, the best things, God's priority things? Hopefully they are. But if you pinpoint any areas that are not of a priority nature, you need to also...

Learn to eliminate—This brings us to the last step in managing your time and your life. It's this: Ask the question, *What can be eliminated from my life at this time that is not a priority?* Life has its "seasons" (as Solomon observed in Ecclesiastes 3:1-8). Today you may be a single woman. Next year you may be married. Or now you may be in the season of childraising. Or you may be like me, in the season of doing all the things I set aside until my children were raised.

The point is, your priorities change. So today, in whatever your situation and season, eliminate those things that don't contribute positively and constructively to God's plan and priorities. Eliminate what does not promote His purposes for your life. There are so many activities that we as women do every day that are not essential. They are discretionary, meaning we can choose to do them or not do them. It makes little or no difference. The call is ours. So, if we are really serious about the better management of our time and our lives, these secondary things must be eliminated.

Just for Today...

Throughout this book we are focusing in this section on a daily key to wisdom, on living out God's timeless principles one day at a time. How do we cultivate lives marked by wisdom? By paying careful attention to time! And the management of our time is another of God's wisdom principles that we must practice today...and extend for a lifetime. So...

❑ Just for today...evaluate your day at day's end. What did you choose to do that was discretionary and could have been eliminated? Make a list to build on so you can identify the "time bandits" that robbed you of a precious day of life. Wisdom is intent on not making the same mistakes twice! So, how could you have better lived this day? Again, if you have a journal, write your answers down...in red ink! You are on assignment from God to use your time and your life for *Him!*

❑ Just for tomorrow...read Titus 2:3-5 and list (grab your journal!) the ten essentials for godly living it contains. This is God's Word to His women, so you'll want to embrace these ten principles as your priorities. Then plan them into all your tomorrows.

❑ Just for this week...set aside a time to evaluate the week and plan for the next one. With your lists of "time bandits" and God's list of ten essential principles, craft a better Plan A for next week. And, by the way, plan on your calendar to do this same exercise at the end of next week. You'll be amazed at your use of time as you continue this drill for the rest of the year. At year's end you will want to praise God for His wisdom and your progress. And, of course, you'll want to evaluate the year and plan for next year.

Seeking a Heart of Wisdom

Wow! We've covered a lot—our time, our lives, our priorities, our purposes! But it's important. The rest of your life is ahead of you. Your life with its minutes, hours, days, and (Lord willing) years is brimming with possibilities. The mark of a woman who is wise in heart is that she enters all her tomorrows with great excitement and enthusiasm. If you and I take heed to God's wisdom regarding our time and our lives, that wise woman will be you and me, my dear sister! Why? Because we have determined, with God's help, to manage our lives by managing our time…one day at a time. And because we are managing our "lives" God's way, we will have the "time" to take advantage of every God-given opportunity that all our tomorrows hold.

I can hardly wait! How about you?

More Wisdom Regarding...
My Time

~ Solomon's Wise Observations on Time ~

There is a right time for everything:
A time to be born; a time to die;
a time to plant; a time to harvest;
a time to kill; a time to heal;
a time to destroy; a time to rebuild;
a time to cry; a time to laugh;
a time to grieve; a time to dance;
a time for scattering stones; a time for gathering stones;
a time to hug; a time not to hug;
a time to find; a time to lose;
a time for keeping; a time for throwing away;
a time to tear; a time to repair;
a time to be quiet; a time to speak up;
a time for loving; a time for hating;
a time for war; a time for peace.
Ecclesiastes 3:1-8[6]

See then that you walk circumspectly,
not as fools but as wise,
redeeming the time, because the days are evil.
Ephesians 5:15-16

Nine-tenths of wisdom consists in
being wise in scheduling time.
—*President Theodore Roosevelt*

What you do today is important because
you are exchanging a day of your life for it.

Each day is a little life,
and our whole life is but a single day repeated.

8

I Need Help with...

My Schedule

God is a gift-giving God. And one of the "gifts" He gave me some time ago was a most special friend with a passion for flower arranging. One piece of life-changing advice this dear woman passed on to me was shared in the context of a wedding. We were both busy at work in the kitchen of the church we attended. I was organizing the wedding reception, and Julie was putting together the floral centerpieces for the reception tables. She had all the fresh flowers she was using organized by size and color and laid out on newspapers spread the full length of the kitchen counter.

And what fantastic centerpieces were coming together before my very eyes! I had never seen anything like them. As Julie busily snipped and stripped, wired and fussed over each stalk and blossom, I verbally admired the dramatic sprays that somehow magically took on a life of their own under the direction of her hands. From the chaos of the mess in the kitchen, beauty was emerging. Finally I asked Julie why her arrangements were so extraordinary. What made them so spectacular? What was her secret?

In just two words, Julie changed my life. She said, "My motto for everything I do is, 'Be bold!' "

Be bold! As we consider our life and the topic of a daily schedule, I want us to keep Julie's motto in mind. I want us to "be bold." I want us to "think bold." And I want us to "live bold" for God. After all, He has given us life in Himself (Ephesians 2:5). He has gifted us to live life for Him (2 Peter 1:3). And He has purposes in mind for our lives (2 Timothy 1:9).

"A List of Projected Operations"

What is a schedule? Technically, a schedule is a list of times and details of recurring events and projected operations. A schedule is also a timed plan for a procedure or project.

As the "Head of Operations" for your life, your relationships, your home, and your work, you, too, need a list for the projected operation of these vital spheres of your life.

Why have a schedule? Every wise woman needs a schedule. Why? First (as we've been discussing) there's your purpose— God's purpose. A schedule helps you fulfill God's purpose for your life...and your day. I love the impassioned words proclaimed by the apostle Paul. When he spoke of God, he added these words—"to whom I belong and whom I serve" (Acts 27:23). To whom do you belong, and who is it that you are serving today? A schedule helps you to live out your purpose of serving *God* and of fulfilling *His* purpose for your life.

Next there's your manner. A schedule helps to bring more discipline into your life, which better enables you to walk in the Spirit and produce spiritual fruit. When there is no schedule and no plan, stress, frustration, and even rage can characterize the gift of 1,440 sparkling minutes God gives to you each day. We don't know what we're doing...but we know things aren't the way we want them to be. That's when the stressful emotions usually kick in. By contrast, with a schedule—a timed plan for a procedure or project—you can flow through "the projected operation" of your day in a calm, orderly, smooth progression.

Then there's the matter of wisdom. A schedule is a mark of wisdom. For instance, consider God's Proverbs 31 woman. Even a brief look at her daily life (Proverbs 31:10-31) gives us a list of priorities and a schedule we can follow. Note them both.

She feared the Lord (verse 30).

She tended her home (verse 27).

She served her community (verse 20).

She got up early (verse 15).

She took care of her family and home first (verse 15).

She stayed busy throughout the day (verse 27).

She worked into the evening (verse 18).

Creating an Arrangement

Think back to my time with Julie, the creator of bold and beautiful floral arrangements. As she explained to me regarding the masterpieces she creates, some flowers are more brilliant in color, more demanding on the eye, and more important to the visual effect of the bouquet. Therefore these major blossoms must be cut tall, stand upright, and be inserted into the arrangement first. Others flowers, though, are softer in color and come next, surrounding the more exciting blossoms. Still others are filler, while some are used for their fragrance. Each bloom, Julie patiently explained, has a place and a purpose.

Before I learned Julie's insights into creating an arrangement of beauty, I used to purchase a cluster of flowers at the grocery store, rip off the cellophane wrapper, and stick it into a vase exactly as it came out of the paper. After Julie's little lesson, though, I began to treat each flower and its placement as important to the whole. I began to learn how to create an arrangement that was bold and beautiful.

Your day, dear reading friend, is to be treated in the same way and with the same carefulness required in creating a breath-taking floral arrangement. You can have a "bunch" of things you need to do that you stick and stuff into God's gift of 24 hours. Or you can lay out and consider all the different tasks you need to take care of, prepare for, and finish, and then thoughtfully and oh-so-painstakingly prioritize and place them in the perfect position in your schedule. Don't you think this second way is the better way? As a woman of wisdom, you must seriously and prayerfully consider the value of each task and the best time for it...including the value of each minute and the best way to use it.

Creating a Schedule

Step 1—What is "the one thing," the most important thing, the central focus, the most brilliant "flower" of your day? That is the question that you must ask first thing, each and every day. Once answered, you then create and build your day around it. You arrange everything else *after* it and *around* it.

And we know what that determinative flower is, don't we? It's *God*. It's your spiritual life—the one thing that makes all the difference in your day. Without setting aside time to cultivate and nurture the all-encompassing priority of your relationship with God, there will be no bold life lived for God. Without it there will be no energy, no purpose, no wisdom, and no joy. "No woman is living at her best who is not living at her best spiritually."[1]

So...first things first—schedule your time with God first.

Step 2—God's list of priorities puts Himself first, then *people*. So now for the second question: Who are the people in your life? Be careful how you answer this one! If you are married and have children, *they* are the priority people in your life, not your sister, best girlfriend, neighbor, or the girls at work or church. This doesn't mean that your friends and ministries don't have a place in your life. But when it comes to your schedule, schedule family first…then other people.

Into the schedule (or the bouquet of your day) go the people in your life. *How* can you serve them and tend to them? *What* can you do for them? What *will* you do for them? And *when* will you do it? Write your plans down and place them into specific time slots on your daily schedule.

Step 3—Many women's lives are filled with failure and frustration because they neglect this most important step in scheduling their days—that is taking into account the *future*. Every woman has events and tasks that loom in the future. Lord willing, these activities will one day arrive, and our job is to be ready for them, prepared for them, even eagerly awaiting them. (That's what the wise woman does—Proverbs 21:5!)

For instance, as I am writing about the scheduling principle, I just took a look at my future. All I can say is, Eek! Here's what I discovered: This book manuscript is due in a few weeks, along with its growth and study guide. My little granddaughter Katie is turning three and needs to be properly honored. My family is having its annual reunion over President's Day weekend. Valentine's Day is coming…and you know what that means! Jim and I need to make travel arrangements to various events this spring. And that's just the tip of the iceberg—the biggies.

The future always looks foreboding and impossible. But (I pray!) I've got these items under control. That simply means I've got some part of the work and preparations for each deadline/birthday/reunion/Valentine's Day scheduled on today's schedule. This practice will be repeated each and every day until the day for each arrives...and hopefully, I will be ready. (And I didn't even mention April 15, the due date for taxes!)

Step 4—And don't forget yourself! Are you trying to lose a pound or two? Are you endeavoring to exercise a little each day? Do you need to pick up the phone and call to enroll in a special class or a Bible study or to make a doctor's or hair appointment? Do you need to pick up a book you're wanting to read? Into the daily schedule these worthy endeavors go.

Step 5—After you've become faithful in planning and scheduling your days, you'll want to graduate to creating a...

- *Weekly schedule*—As you create your plan for your weeks, pay attention to *horizontal scheduling* (the same things every day at the same times...like getting up, reading your Bible, exercising, preparing meals, your daily good house-keeping chores, and planning your next day).

   Then go to work on your *vertical scheduling* (blocking off large time slots during a day...like three hours to clean your house or work on a correspondence course or run your errands).

- *Monthly schedule*—This basically becomes an appoint-ment calendar-at-a-glance. Key dates, meetings, and commitments are noted so there are no surprises. This practice also brings the big picture of your year down to a smaller, more manageable slice of reality. Now, whose birthday is this month?

- *Yearly schedule*—This schedule is a reflection of the flow of your life. It includes birthdays, holidays, family com-mitments, medical reminders, church events, the school calendar, wedding dates, graduations...and always those deadlines!

   My yearly calendar includes not only my book deadlines, but my husband's as well. Both our ministry commitments are written in, plus our anniversary date and Jim's birthday. You'll find our daughters' birthdays there...and now their husbands' birthdays as well (and their anniversaries)...plus those of five grandchildren. Every holiday and special date is marked off along with my family's annual reunion.

Just for Today...

As you can see, scheduling is a necessity. It's a mirror of your life. It's a tool for improvement. And it's a wand for accomplishment! Think about the creation of the world. God had a schedule...from before the foundation of the world. He knew exactly what He would create each day that first most glorious week of the history of all creation. It was a true masterpiece! And He knew He would rest on the seventh day. How about you? How's your masterpiece looking?

❏ Just for today...create a schedule—even a bad one! Spend the first ten to fifteen minutes of your day creating a plan for the day and putting that plan on your daily schedule. And remember—*any* schedule is better than *no* schedule!

❏ Just for tomorrow...seek to make a better schedule. Determine to make tomorrow a better day than yesterday. And don't forget to ask God for His wisdom (James 1:5)!

Also schedule a visit to an office supply store. Take time to look at the different types of planners, calendars, and scheduling tools. If you don't have one of these devices, purchase one that will get you started. If you already have one, see if there is something better than what you are using or that will complement it.

❑ Just for this week...make a schedule first thing every day. Determining a schedule and imposing deadlines give urgency to activities that might otherwise drag. Keep your journal handy, too, because you'll want to record your amazing progress! A complete makeover is in motion!

Seeking a Heart of Wisdom

As I think about the days of our lives, I can't help but feel an urgency. Dear sister, I'll say it again—all you and I have is today! Only this one day! Therefore as we seek a heart of wisdom, we must pray over our day of potential, we must pray through it, and we must pray at the end of it. How desperately our desperately wicked hearts (Jeremiah 17:9) need God's clear direction and wisdom for our one day! Without it we won't care about the day...or about others. We'll indulge ourselves, shirk our work, and spend God's golden minutes on the foolishness of this world. And, as the saying goes, You cannot kill time without injuring eternity.

So we weak and fleshly mortals have no hope but to pray! We must pray and ask God for *His* wisdom, *His* guidance, and *His* plan for the use of our day...which is *His*. There is no other way our day will be used for *His* purposes and to *His* glory. And there is no other way to bless others and move forward and "press toward the goal for the prize of the upward call of God in Christ Jesus" (Philippians 3:14). So, as we think about our schedules for the day, let's join the ranks of God's corps of wise servants. Let's *ask* God for His wisdom—"If any of you lacks wisdom, let him *ask* of God...and it will be given to him" (James 1:5).

What's in a Day?

Just for today, I will…

Like Enoch—walk in daily fellowship
with my Heavenly Father.

Like Abraham—trust implicitly in my God.

Like Job—be patient under all circumstances.

Like Joseph—turn my back on all seductive advances.

Like Moses—choose to suffer rather than
enjoy the pleasures of sin.

Like Caleb and Joshua—refuse to be discouraged
because of numbers.

Like Gideon—advance, even though my friends are few.

Like David—lift up my eyes to the hills
from which comes my help.

Like Jehoshaphat—prepare my heart to seek the Lord.

Like Daniel—commune with God at all times
and in all places.

Like Andrew—strive to lead others to Christ.

Like Stephen—manifest a forgiving spirit
toward all who seek my hurt.

Like Paul—forget those things that are behind
and press forward.[2]

More Wisdom Regarding...
My Schedule

Ponder the path of your feet,
and let all your ways be established.
Proverbs 4:26

Commit your works to the LORD,
and your thoughts will be established.
Proverbs 16:3

A man's heart plans his way,
but the LORD directs his steps.
Proverbs 16:9

The plans of the diligent lead surely to plenty,
but those of everyone who is hasty, surely to poverty.
Proverbs 21:5

Let all things be done decently and in order.
1 Corinthians 14:40

"What makes a home?"
I asked my little boy.
And this is what he said,
"You, Mother,
And when Father comes,
Our table set all shiny,
And my bed,
And, Mother, I think it's home
Because we love each other."

You who are old and wise,
What would you say
If you were asked the question?
Tell me, pray?

Thus simply as a little child, we learn
A home is made from love.
Warm as the golden hearthfire on the floor,
A table and a lamp for light,
And smooth white beds at night—
Only the old sweet fundamental things.
And long ago I learned—
Home may be near, home may be far,
But it is anywhere that love
And a few plain household treasures are.[1]

9

I Need Help with...
My Home

Tomorrow will be the one-month anniversary of my dear sweet mother's death at age 93. I still can't believe it! Between Jim and me, she was our last living parent. And now, as of New Year's Eve, she is gone. It is a sore loss.

Yet, as I've been reminiscing this past month on my growing-up years, there is no doubt that my mother marked my life forever as a "home" maker. Although she was a serious and dedicated schoolteacher by day, she was a homemaker *par excellence* at all other times. She loved to sew by hand and by machine. She personally and artistically placed every object in our home to create a sight worthy of a still-life painter's brush! She groomed and tended a plethora of house plants that brought beauty, life, and freshness to our small house. She set the table for every meal with great care—a different tablecloth or attractive placements, cloth napkins (hand sewn, or rather, in her case, magically "whipped up" out of leftover fabrics). She loved her blue willow dishes, and even served the catsup in a small attractive glass bowl with a tiny silver spoon. (No paper plates on our table! And no bottles or jars either!) Every wall, too, was hung with her beautiful and fine needlework, lovingly sewn by her own hands.

Well, I could truly go on and on about my mom (and I'm sure you could do the same about your mother!). But I shocked myself early this morning as I came down the stairs to begin my new day and caught sight of our breakfast table. There it was, completely set with beautiful woven placemats, every mat with a full place setting of dishes and silverware, complete with a bright cloth napkin in a napkin ring, a live succulent plant as a centerpiece imbedded in a wreath of candles and entwined with twinkle lights. The side table, too, was laden with a bowl of fruit as if a master were about to paint it. I instantly had two thoughts. The first was, *I can't help myself! It's so deeply ingrained in me! I love the beauty of simple things set with care!* And my second was, *Thank you, my dear departed mother! I love you and thank God for you!*

A Home Must Be Built

Two of my favorite proverbs (well, actually four) show me the wisdom of what my mom put into practice regarding her home and home-making. I think as you read them you will clearly see that "building" or making a home is a mark of wisdom for every woman.

- ❧ Wisdom has built her house (Proverbs 9:1).

- ❧ Every wise woman builds her house (Proverbs 14:1).

- ❧ Through wisdom a house is built, and by understanding it is established; by knowledge the rooms are filled with all precious and pleasant riches (Proverbs 24:3-4).

- ❧ She watches over the ways of her household (Proverbs 31:27).

What these God-breathed scriptures communicate to you and me as women seeking His wisdom for our everyday needs is that it's important—and necessary—for us to focus on our home, on the place where we live. Married or single, we live somewhere. And that somewhere is to be a home. And that home must be "built" and watched over.

So, my dear reading friend, where is your heart when it comes to the Home-making and Home-building and Home-watching Departments? Do you even care? Even a little bit? A better question is, Do you care passionately? So much so that you are investing your God-given talents and time in carrying out this most important assignment from Him? I know it takes a little doing, but here are a few things that help my heart stay focused on home.

Prayer—lifts the work of home-making out of the physical realm and transports it into the spiritual realm. Prayer moves our hearts to accept God's will for our lives. Prayer lines up our desires with God's good and acceptable and perfect will and wisdom for us. So pray! Pray when you get up. Pray as you plan your work. Pray that your work will bless the people under your roof. Pray as you do your work. Pray to finish your work. Pray to do your work as unto the Lord (Colossians 3:23). Pray when you are done. And, as you admire the awesome results of your handiwork, pray a prayer of praise and thanksgiving to your all-wise God. Prayer sweetens—and empowers!—every task.

Resolution—always helps. Indeed, it's needful! So purpose in your heart (and in prayer!) to faithfully live out God's wise plan for you. Even if creating a home is not the burning desire of your heart, purpose to follow God's will, no matter what. Then trust Him for the blessings He chooses to "pour out" (Malachi 3:10) and send your way as you obey. Watch for them, wait for them, and write them down when they come. As the psalmist instructs, "Bless the LORD, O my soul, and *forget not* all His benefits" (Psalm 103:2). A journal helps!

Presence—your presence—at home is how a home is built, maintained, and enjoyed. It's true that the easiest way to feel at home is to be there. And the more you and I (the home-makers) are there, the more we see, the more we care, and the more time we have to care for our homes. My husband and I travel together—a lot! But the truth is, we are two homing pigeons. People are so gracious and thoughtful to offer us extended stays, penthouse apartments overlooking a beach, island layovers or getaways for a little R&R, and guided day-tours of their wonderful cities. But the truth is that our hearts are always leaning toward home. So, like a pair of homing pigeons, home we fly! Wherever we are, we can't wait to get home! Don't get me wrong. We greatly enjoy what we do in ministry to and with God's family everywhere. And we sincerely love those we meet and serve with. And we are truly grateful for all the loving gestures made by Christians everywhere. But, for us, *home* is where our hearts are! The age-old quip is true—Dry bread at home is better than roast meat abroad!

Time—is key to caring for your home…or anything else! As I wrote regarding a garden in *God's Wisdom for Little Girls*,[2]

> The garden of God's little girl—how grand!
> It began with a dream, a prayer, and a plan.
> Nothing this splendid just happens, we know;
> It takes time and care for flowers to grow.

We both know that the truth in this simple rhyme applies to a home too, don't we? In fact, we could substitute the word *home* for *garden*. So dedicate time to taking care of your home. Time each day. And as you begin to taste the pleasing fruits of your labor, you'll want to commit even more time to your little place called *home*. And soon you'll reap the payoff for your minutes spent. You'll have something grand! And remember, nothing grand or splendid *just happens*, you know. It takes *time* and care for a home to grow.

Do you yet have your dream, your prayer, and your plan? Then all you need is some time!

A Home Is Built with Care

Please be sure you understand that when I speak of "building" a home, I am not talking about spending money. No, our focus is on the care, for that's how a home is built. What does it take to build a home? As the proverbs several pages back stated, it is by wisdom, understanding, and knowledge (Proverbs 24:3-4). It is by ordinary prudence and discretion. It is by skillful management with intelligent and biblical principles.

So Step 1 would definitely be to possess a blueprint for building a home. (And you do—God's blueprint is right in the Bible). And you need a plan. (And you have that too—God's plan is right in the Bible. He has revealed it.)

Step 2 would then be to work out God's plan. It's true that one's efforts are usually crowned with success. And it is by your prayer efforts and your work efforts (and by God's good grace!) that your home is built, established, and furnished, honors Him, and blesses others. Indeed, when you follow God's perfect plan, your home will be "filled with all precious and pleasant riches" (Proverbs 24:4), "with rare and beautiful treasures" (NASB).

Riches and treasures like what? Like love, joy, peace, goodness. Like an abundance of spiritual qualities. Like a patient, loving calmness that ministers to body and soul. Like words that are "sweetness to the soul and health to the bones" (Proverbs 16:24). Upon such wealth your home will be founded and furnished when you follow God's timeless principles. As a scholar-of-old put it, "The wise woman builds her house upon piety and prudence."[3]

Just for Today…

Good habits are purposefully formed. And that's what you want to do today…and every day—form good habits, even (and especially!) in the area of caring for your home. Why? Because what you are at home is what you are. So…

❏ Just for today…spend five minutes praying specifically about your home and home-making. Pray through the scriptures we've discussed in this chapter. Affirm to God your desire to be the wise woman who builds and watches over her home. Then walk through each room. Spend the few minutes that it takes to ensure they are clean, tidy, pleasant, welcoming, and comfortable. Make sure they have a fussed-over feeling. As you pass through each room, think about and pray for each person who occupies that room. Consider their needs. Remember the little guy in the poem at the beginning of this chapter, how he remarked on the *people* at home first— "You, Mother…and then Father." Then he went on to convey the importance of the *place*—the set table, his bed (complete with smooth white sheets), the warmth communicated by the simplest of things…like a table and a lamp.

❏ Just for tomorrow…repeat the daily exercise above. Now add to these gestures of love by thinking about each meal for the day. Consider the health of those in your household, their need for energy and nutrition. Plan out three meals and snacks for each person (or two meals if no one is there for lunch or if someone eats lunch out). And don't forget to include yourself. After all, it's conceivable that *you* need the most energy of all! Why? Because *you* are the home-maker. Without you and your efforts, the whole thing topples!

❏ Just for this week…take notice of how you feel as you reap the rewards of "building" and making your home. And if you have a journal, jot down your impressions. One feeling you'll probably experience is some tiredness. But oh, will it be worth it! Imagine…loving your home for an entire week, fussing over the people you love and the place you love for seven whole days, tending to the little touches that transform a house into a home! Be careful to also keep a list of improvements you need to make—not only in your house but in your house-keeping. Note what it was that kept you from doing your tasks, that drained you of the energy needed to take care of your high and noble calling of home-building. Was it food (the lack of, the excess of, the choice of)? Was it the television? The telephone? Pinpointing the culprits will make next week a better one. One more suggestion—I once heard someone say, "You become what you read." So purchase or borrow a book on cleaning your home. Learn a method that saves you time and gets the job done quickly.

The truth about all our home-making efforts is that we will be at them for a very long time, right up until the minute we are no longer able! Wherever we live, that place is our home, and that place becomes the stage upon which we live out this most important, rewarding, and meaningful role. Just think of the scores of people you will bless, not to mention the sheer joy you will receive from your home-sweet-home!

Seeking a Heart of Wisdom

I feel like a cheerleader on the sidelines of your life, putting all my energy into cheering you on. My encouraging chants for you and your home-making go something like this: "Do it! Build it! Love it!… And then do it! Build it! And love it some more!"

But there is one final cheer I want to pass on to you—Pass it on! If you have daughters and/or daughters-in-law, or if you know younger women in your church, pass on what you know and are learning about taking care of your place. When I visit my two daughters' homes, I am amazed by their skills, by the beauty they create, by the order I witness in their homes. Why, just yesterday I dropped by to pick up Courtney's little Jacob to take him to his church Cubbies meeting. And what did I see? Courtney's table was set with a red, white, and blue tablecloth (yes, she's a Navy wife through and through!) with placemats for each person. The dishes were already set on the mats. Two tiny candles with little lamp shades were set on either end of the table. And a sprig of evergreen she had plucked from a tree in the backyard brought its fresh beauty and the fresh scent of pine into her cozy home.

And I'll never forget my Katherine's first Thanksgiving as a married woman! She invited Jim and me to a sit-down dinner of turkey done "Martha Stewart style," artistically arranged and served on a large pewter platter. And there was the table… resplendent with a seasonal runner gracing the length of her table. Katherine had also spread variegated gourds up and down the length of the table, many of them cut out so that lit candles were sticking up out of them. She delighted in using her wedding dishes, silverware, and goblets. To this day I never enter her house without seeing her table decorated in a stunning way.

And then I think of my mother…passing on her passion for home-making to me. And then I think of my daughters…and that's when I hope and pray and thank God that maybe, just maybe(!), I have passed on the same passion to them! And then I think of little Taylor Jane and Katie, just four and three years old, coming along behind my daughters…

As I said, pass it on!

More Wisdom Regarding...
My Home

Wisdom has built her house,
she has hewn out her seven pillars;
she has slaughtered her meat
she has mixed her wine,
she has also furnished her table.
Proverbs 9:1-2

Every wise woman builds her house,
but the foolish pulls it down with her hands.
Proverbs 14:1

Through wisdom a house is built,
and by understanding it is established;
by knowledge the rooms are filled
with all precious and pleasant riches.
Proverbs 24:3-4

She watches over the ways of her household,
and does not eat the bread of idleness.
Proverbs 31:27

The older women [are to]...
admonish the young women
to [be] homemakers.
Titus 2:3-5

God's Wisdom for...
Your Family Life

*D*o you take this man
to be your lawfully wedded husband,
to have and to hold from this day forward,
for better, for worse,
for richer, for poorer,
in sickness and in health,
to love and to cherish,
till death you do part,
according to God's holy ordinance?[1]

10

I Need Help with...

My Marriage

*J*ust this morning my sweet Jim remarked, "Do you realize we are on the downhill side of the year, moving toward 38 years of marriage?" As the the two of us talked about this startling feat, we wondered, How did 38 years together happen? How did we do it? And what have we learned?

How did it happen? Obviously, both Jim and I wholeheartedly acknowledge—100 percent—that an almost four-decade marriage must be attributed to God's good grace and an untold abundance of His transforming power! Whenever we consider our bumpy beginnings and the near dissolution of our marriage, we can only fall before Him in complete adoration and thanksgiving.

And how did we do it? I'm chuckling as I think of the obvious answer—we did a lot of it the hard way! But seriously, we have earnestly tried to do it *God's* way. Once we became a Christian family (after eight years of some very rocky road!), we found in the Bible what God had to say about marriage. From that point on we sought to follow the timeless principles for a married couple set down by the Designer of marriage.

And what have we learned? I'm chuckling again as this answer pops into my head—a lot! Yes, we've learned an awful lot…and there's still more that we are learning every day! But here's a little of what we now know.

Ten Timeless Principles for a Wife

As you read through these principles, keep several things in mind. If you are married, whether to a Christian or non-Christian mate, these are guidelines that will help you be a better wife—God's kind of wife. They provide biblical roles and godly goals for you. If you are not married, please also take note of the principles. Why? Because you never know when *you* will be the one who can help another woman…just because you know God's timeless wisdom for wives. In the past, I helped to train college-age and career women for short-term summer missions trips. One key thing our church wanted these single women to be able to teach and communicate was God's plan for women in the church and in the home as wives and mothers. You see, God's timeless principles work for every wife…everywhere.

1. *Work as a team*—If your husband watches any sports on TV, then you are well aware of the importance of teamwork. And never is this basic principle more important than in marriage. Teamwork in marriage requires the husband and wife to take up their tandem roles of leading and following. It is the practice that makes a marriage work. God asks husbands to lead and wives to follow (1 Corinthians 11:3). So, your husband is called to lead, and you, dear wife, are called to follow. For now, just hang on to this principle!

2. *Learn to communicate*—Perhaps this is a part of the "how" of Principle #1. To function as a team, you and your husband must communicate. That means you must learn *how* to communicate. More specifically, you must learn how to communicate with *your* husband. He's not a woman, so communication with him will not be carried on like it is with your sister, mother,

or girlfriends. You'll need to pay attention to *time*—when is the best time to talk to your mate? You'll need to pay attention to *tone*—what is the best tone of voice to use with your husband? And you'll need to pay attention to *tongue*—what is the most gracious, sensible, and reasonable choice of words when talking things over with your hubbie?

The Bible is clear on its keys to communication. Your words are to be...

> ...soft (a soft and gentle answer turns away wrath—Proverbs 15:1),
>
> ...sweet (the sweetness of the lips increases learning—Proverbs 16:21),
>
> ...suitable (pleasant words are health to the body—Proverbs 16:24),
>
> ...scant (in the multitude of words one cannot avoid sinning—Proverbs 10:19), and
>
> ...slow (be swift to hear, slow to speak, and slow to anger—James 1:19).

3. *Enjoy intimacy*—Not only is verbal communication a key principle to marriage, but physical communication is too. Sexual intimacy in marriage was designed by God. Why? Here are some why's and how's.

> *Proclaimed*—God proclaimed that you and your husband are to leave your parents and be joined together as "one flesh" (Genesis 2:24-25). God intends the two of you—two incomplete individual people—to come together in marriage and sexual intimacy and become a new whole, complete in each other.

Procreation—God desires that the oneness created between a husband and wife in sexual intimacy result in another generation of offspring who will continue to multiply and fill the earth (Genesis 1:27-28).

Pleasure—Sexual intimacy was also designed by God to provide pleasure for both partners (Proverbs 5:15-19). This pleasure thrives as each spouse chooses to serve the other and determines not to deprive one other (1 Corinthians 7:5).

Purity—Sex within marriage is pure (Hebrews 13:4) and provides power against sexual temptation, contributing positively to the purity of both husband and wife (1 Corinthians 7:2).

Partnership—Each marriage partner has a God-given assignment to satisfy the other's physical needs and to see that their own needs are satisfied too (1 Corinthians 7:3-4).

Protection—Sex in marriage is a safeguard against lust, temptation, and Satan's alluring, worldly tactics (1 Corinthians 7:5).

4. *Manage money*—My husband writes and teaches on marriage, and one thing I've heard him often say is that beneath almost every argument between a couple is some issue over finances. It's true that money—the use of it and the lack of it!—can produce tension. So what can you as a wife do? It helps if you are content in your heart (Philippians 4:11-13). Contentment enables you to look at something and say in your heart, "I can live with it or without it. It doesn't make any difference to me! I'm content in the Lord." That attitude will go a long way in the Money Department. Plus the area of finances creates an opportunity to practice patience, to grow in your trust of the Lord, and to implement the good communication skills we've

been talking about with your husband. You should also determine to grow in your understanding of money management, budgeting, saving, basic bookkeeping, and giving. Choose a book on the subject…and start growing!

5. *Keep up the home*—Married or single, your home is an indicator of your spiritual maturity and a direct reflection of your care and character. And if you are married, home is the focal point for your marriage and family. Its condition also sends a loud message and leaves a visual impression on friends, neighbors, and those at church about you, your husband, and the attention you pay (or don't pay) to the people and place that make up your home. What a vital area for a wife! Treat the upkeep and atmosphere of your home with utmost care. Become a home lover (Titus 2:5). A lot is riding on your desire to keep up your home. Make it your aim to look well to the ways of your household (Proverbs 31:27).

6. *Raise your children*—Here's another area that requires some good communication. The typical scene goes something like this—generally Mom spends time at home with the little darlings, training and disciplining away…and then Dad comes home and proceeds to train and discipline in another way…or not at all! Childraising is an area of potential friction and, once again, calls for good communication. The goal is to know what the Bible says about childraising, talk it over with your husband, agree on a plan for raising and training your children…and then be prepared to revise the plan often.

Why? Because things change! You are growing and learning, the children are developing and moving from stage to stage, and the outside influences of others (friends, school surroundings, neighbors, workmates at their jobs, sports teammates and coaches) are appearing almost daily! Yes, you'll be talking with your husband about these "things" a lot(!), maybe even every day…and for a long time! So don't forget God's keys to good communication (see Principle #2). You are to train your children and bring them up in the ways of the Lord (Proverbs 22:6 and Ephesians 6:4), and that assignment will require that you and your husband communicate, agree, move forward together, and adjust all along the way.

7. *Make time for fun*—Jim and I work hard…*very* hard! But we make it a point to make time for fun. We try to regularly schedule in recreation and time spent on our hobbies and interests, whether joint or individual ones. We adore our walks in the woods, kayaking as a couple, and boating when the weather permits. Fun for us is scouring flea markets and junk stores for used "treasures." Fun is walking through the lobbies of famous hotels we could never afford to stay in. (And *real* fun is to have coffee in such a hotel, to sit and sip and pretend…and enjoy the magnificent ambience for the price of two cups of coffee!) What is fun for you and your husband? Is it jigsaw puzzles? Bicycling? Do you perhaps need to do a little more communicating with your husband on when and how and what you can do to make time for fun?

8. *Serve the Lord*—Nothing is more healthy (and rewarding!) for a couple than serving the Lord together. Along with your regular worship at church, such service is healthy because it focuses the two of you outside of yourselves and onto bettering the lives of others. As a couple, Jim and I have set up, cleaned up, and washed up more times and more dishes at the church than we can count! We've stuffed, assembled, painted, planted, cooked, moved, visited, given, served, hosted…you name it, we've done it in both our church and our community. Now, how can you and your husband serve the Lord and His people?

9. *Reach out to others*—Hand in hand with serving the Lord is reaching out to others. What a wonderful privilege you and your husband have to work together as you minister to your

friends and neighbors! By seeking to apply the other nine of these timeless principles for marriage, the two of you can model the reality of Christ and a Christian marriage before an unbelieving world. As you open up your heart and your home in hospitality to others and their children, you demonstrate Christ's love to all who enter through your doors.

Just for Today…

There you have it—nine (I've saved one for later!) out of ten timeless principles for you and your marriage! They provide a lot for you to think about, don't they? And to apply…because nothing as grand as a God-honoring marriage ever happens without work. Each principle is a part of God's plan for strengthening your marriage. So pick out several and begin to make them a part of your marriage. And be prepared—more than likely, you will notice a change in not only your attitude but also in your husband's!

❏ Just for today…review the nine principles above and the one that follows. Write out all ten on a 3" x 5" card. Carry them with you and revisit them often, even every hour. Do as Solomon said: In essence, "Bind them around your neck, write them on the tablet of your heart" (Proverbs 3:3). Then go a step further and identify the one principle that troubles you most, that causes you to stumble, that is perhaps a source of contention between you and your husband. Pray, dear one…and purpose to zero in on that principle by applying God's wisdom to your life and marriage.

❏ Just for tomorrow…get the old grey matter perking! Can you cook your husband's favorite meal? Can you drop a little love note into his sack lunch or slip it into his pocket or briefcase? Can you think of three things you can compliment him on…and can you verbalize them?

Can you plan a romantic evening together after the children are in bed? Think! Plan! Then act!

❏ Just for this week…read through this acrostic on marriage every day, paying attention to its instruction and your heart's response.

M - make your marriage a priority.

A - ask God for wisdom.

R - respect an honor your husband.

R - realize marriage is a book with many "chapters"!

I - invest large amounts of time in your marriage.

A - adhere to God's keys to communication.

G - grow in your understanding of your role as a wife.

E - enjoy your mate and God's gift of marriage!

Seeking a Heart of Wisdom

And now for the greatest of all keys to wisdom! As you seek a heart of wisdom and as you seek to better your marriage, be sure you…

10. *Grow in the Lord*—The greatest influence you can have on your marriage is through your spiritual growth. As you grow in the Lord, you become a tremendous support to your husband as you are available to listen and give wise counsel. Even if yours is a difficult marriage and even in difficult times, your faithful attention to growing in the Lord will give you the wisdom for handling problems. Your spiritual growth permeates every area of your life

and is vital to your husband and to the well-being of your marriage and family. I'm sure you, like I, want to be like the woman in Proverbs 31 who feared and revered the Lord and was highly praised and appreciated by her husband (Proverbs 31:28-30). The best way to be a godly wife—and a wise one!—is to continually grow in the Lord.

More Wisdom Regarding... My Marriage

And the LORD God said,
"It is not good that man should be alone;
I will make him a helper comparable to him."
Genesis 2:18

Therefore a man shall leave his father and mother
and be joined to his wife,
and they shall become one flesh.
Therefore what God has joined together,
let not man separate.
Genesis 2:24 and Matthew 19:5-6

Two are better than one,
because they have a good reward for their labor.
For if they fall, one will lift up his companion.
Ecclesiastes 4:9-10

Let the wife see that she respects her husband.
Ephesians 5:33

Let the husband render to his wife the affection due her,
and likewise also the wife to her husband.
1 Corinthians 7:3

A mother whose heart is obedient to God, full of faith,
and "dedicated" to the Lord and to her family
will dedicate her time, energy, and life
to taking full advantage of the opportunity to train her
children and to fulfilling her parental duty to do so.
—*Elizabeth George*

11

I Need Help with...
My Children

During the many years of our marriage my husband, Jim, has spent a great deal of time away from our home. His involvement with missions, his monthly duties in the U.S. Army Reserves, his responsibilities as pastor of visitation, evangelism, and outreach, plus his night classes at seminary and teaching in a Bible institute, added up to many absences...which added up to my often being "home alone" with our two daughters during their formative years.

So what's a young mom to do?

Wisdom from a Godly Mother

As I searched for help on how to handle my two little preschoolers when their dad was away, I turned to reading the many biographies of Ruth Graham, wife of Billy Graham. I had heard that during some of the years of their marriage, the great evangelist Billy Graham was away from home for months at a time. Surely Mrs. Graham had practical wisdom she could give me for those times when my Jim was gone!

And so I read. And as I read, I learned...that Mrs. Graham was a lover of the book of Proverbs...that she read Proverbs daily...that she gleaned from the Proverbs many principles for raising her children...that she kept her Bible, opened to the Proverbs, on the kitchen table all day every day...that she visited the kitchen table often each day to seek God's wisdom from His book of wisdom whenever she needed divine insight for handling her five children without the help or input or direction of her husband.

Wisdom from God

Taking a page out of Mrs. Graham's book, a mother who had gone before me, I turned to my Bible. More specifically, I turned to the book of Proverbs, just as Ruth Graham had. Each day when I read the "Proverb for the Day" (as we discussed in our chapter on "My Bible"), I specifically looked for proverbs that spoke of mothers and mothering, of parents and parenting, of children and childraising. To this day, the verses I found are all clearly marked in my Bible (although the decades have definitely dulled the pen markings!). They guided my daily life then as a young mom with a houseful of little tykes and toddlers. And they are still a living part of me as my two daughters, now young moms with preschoolers, are using the same principles!

So, if you're a mom in need of wisdom for raising your children (and what mom isn't!), here's the first four of what I call...

Ten Timeless Principles for Childraising

1. *Teach your children*—Not only does this principle for mothers come first in the Proverbs (1:8), but it comes often! I personally counted at least 20 times some form of parental teaching is mentioned in the book of Proverbs.

God is not expecting you to have a teaching degree, credentials, or experience. But He is most definitely expecting you to teach your children! In fact, teaching almost appears to be the Number One duty of a Christian parent. The Bible instructs, if you love your children, discipline them (Proverbs 13:24). But it also indicates that, if you love your children, *teach* them. And like discipline, the earlier the better!

I would also say, "Teach them, no matter what!" Moms tell me all the time, "But my children don't want to have devotions. They don't want to sit and listen to me read the Bible or Bible storybooks."

Dear mom, my answer is always the same—"Give your children what they need, not what they want." You're the mom. You're the adult. You know what's best and what wisdom will be needed in the future. Your faithful teaching of your children gives them a base of information (God's truth) from which they can live their lives (God's way). Your teaching equips them to function throughout life with wisdom, thus avoiding many mistakes and heartbreaks. Therefore the wise mother daily makes sure that her children "hear the instruction of…the law" or *Torah*, meaning the law of God, the Word of God (Proverbs 1:8 and 6:20).

2. *Train your children*—"Train up a child in the way he should go, and when he is old he will not depart from it" (Proverbs 22:6). That's God's Word to your heart, precious mom. So my thinking goes like this—*God says to train them, therefore I train them!*

The usual interpretation of this proverb is that if a parent trains a child properly, that child will choose the path of God in later life. Of course there are exceptions. But the principle still stands. So, first of all, we mothers obediently, by faith, train our children. And we train them first *in God's way*. From that point on, we also train them along the lines of their natural talents and individual inclinations or bents.

And what does "training" require of a mom? Most definitely it requires *a heart of obedience*, a heart that heeds God's command to the mother to do the work of training.

But it also requires *a heart of faith*. As God's mothers, we have to believe that, no matter how dark and discouraging things get or how many mysterious, heartbreaking turns the parenting path takes, our teaching is important...just because God says it is.

And it takes *a heart of dedication*. In fact, that is one of the translations of the word *train*—"dedicate" your child and your house and household to the Lord,[1] and when the child is old, he will not depart from Him.

So no matter what—no matter what the obstacles, no matter what the lack of "pay-off," no matter how tired you are, no matter if there isn't even a glimmer of hope, no matter if your diligent teaching and training seems to be making no difference, a mother whose heart is obedient, full of faith, and "dedicated" to the Lord and to her family will dedicate her time, energy, and life to taking full advantage of the opportunity to train her children and to fulfill her parental duty to do so.

3. *Instruct them*—That's the instruction of Proverbs 10:1: "A wise son makes a glad father, but a foolish son is the grief of his mother." (As one commentator interjects, "Every son may turn out to be a Paul or a Judas, with all that means by way of joy or grief."[2]) And so, what wisdom, we wonder, should a mother and father pass on to their children so that they become wise and not foolish? Solomon points specifically to instruction in the area of work.

> He who deals with a slack hand becomes poor, but the hand of the diligent makes one rich. He who gathers in summer is a wise son, but he who sleeps in harvest is a son who causes shame (Proverbs 10:4-5).

Here Solomon is saying that a wise adult is one who has overcome laziness and carelessness and has learned to be diligent and aggressive in his or her work. A wise person knows when to work and how to work, when to pour it on and when to relax, how to seize the day and the opportunities it brings, how to begin a project, how to make steady progress, and how to finish. By following the biblical work ethic, the wise one experiences the sweet taste of success and the rewards of diligent labor.

Therefore, wise and diligent mother, teach your children diligence versus laziness, to work versus to shirk, to finish versus to merely dream and dawdle, to march versus to meander, to focus versus to dabble. And just how does a wise mom move her child in this direction? By...

...communicating clearly what the chore or work or job is that must be done,

...assigning work that is age-appropriate,

...giving specific instructions about what is expected and any timelines or deadlines involved,

...training and showing her child how to do the job,

...insisting that the work meet a set standard,

...requiring that a job be done again if it doesn't meet the set standard,

...reviewing instructions each time a job is given,

...making sure the job is finished,

...asking for a verbal report,

...checking it out herself,

...fine-tuning the "loose ends,"

...rewarding (with praise, with applause, with smiles and hugs or high-fives, with a break, with bragging to others, with a handwritten note of praise on the pillow or desk, with a star on a poster or with car privileges, depending on age, with food as in "We'll have snacktime after you've put your toys away," with fun as in "We'll go to the park or go swimming..." or "You can go visit your friends...when you've finished your homework").

Perhaps our diligent efforts in teaching our children a strong work ethic will lead them to one day declare along with John Wesley, the founder of Methodism and a man marked by his dedication to God and to hard work, "Leisure and I have parted company. I am resolved to be busy till I die.[3]

4. *Correct them*—There's no way to miss this loud message from the Bible! Indeed, the book of Proverbs shouts it to every parent, "He who spares his rod hates his [child], but he who loves him disciplines him promptly" (13:24). "Chasten your son while there is hope" (19:18) (and I like to imagine an exclamation point of urgency here!). In correcting our children we are actually following in the footsteps of our heavenly Father, "for whom the LORD loves He corrects, just as a father the son in whom he delights" (3:12).

And why do we correct our beloved children? First and foremost, because God says we should. Again, Proverbs cries out and commands, "Do not withhold correction from a child" (23:13). Also because "foolishness is bound up in the heart of a child, but the rod of correction will drive it far from him" (22:15). "The rod and reproof give wisdom, but a child left to himself brings shame to his mother" (29:15).

Dear mom, it's hard to grasp—and even harder to follow through—but we actually do our children a disservice when we fail to correct and direct them. You see, when we fail to discipline, we are actually choosing to raise a fool, to sentence him or her to a life of pain, uncontrolled emotions, stupidity, agony, and harsh consequences. In a nutshell then, God's wisdom for mothers says...

- do discipline your children,

- do discipline early in their lives,

- do discipline faithfully and consistently, and

- do discipline out of a heart of love.

Of course your children will protest, cry, squirm, argue, and emote! That's normal. So count on it…and prepare for it (something else a keen mom does!). But remember that a wise mother doesn't let such opposition unnerve her or rock her decision to correct wrong behaviors. Solomon encourages us that, while the child may cry, "he will not die" (23:13)!

Just for Today…

Teaching. Training. Instructing. Correcting. Sounds like a lifelong challenge, doesn't it? And it is! But, like all wisdom, these skills are gained one day at a time. So what can you do…just for today? I'll include more suggestions at the end of our second chapter on being a wise mother, but here are a few quick in-and-out applications.

❏ Just for today…pick a time, a place, and a portion of the Bible to read aloud to and with your children.

❏ Just for tomorrow…prepare yourself to follow the list of "instructions" on page 125 for training your children in the fine art of working and in diligence.

❏ Just for this week…talk about correcting your children with your husband. If there is no father in the family, seek the counsel of your pastor or an older woman. Also visit your Christian bookstore and choose one book on these frightening-but-necessary principles of childraising.

Seeking a Heart of Wisdom

I love every mother of children who range from babies to high schoolers. In fact, I love all women. But somehow this group of mothers is so refreshing. Why? Because they are so teachable. There is nothing proud about them. And there is nothing lazy about them. No, there is a definite need to know! There's a hunger for help. There's a quest for information. They are truly *in* the race and *running* the race (indeed, every minute of every day!). They live every second where the rubber meets the road. Theirs is a day-in, day-out struggle to discover godly wisdom, methods, skills, and practices as they seek to raise the world's—and God's—next generation. They truly have hearts that are seeking wisdom—God's wisdom for them as His mothers.

Are you, precious reader, one of these need-to-know mothers? Oh, how I pray for you! And oh, how I pray that what I've shared from God's Word gives you the courage to continue on, to get up just one more time, just one more day, to look up to our Lord for His strength and wisdom (Proverbs 3:6 and James 1:5), and to persevere by faith, knowing that you are doing what is right because God asks it of you. Take heart, and take up God's calling to you!

Or perhaps, my dear reading friend, you are older and wondering, *Well, this chapter has nothing for me! I've already raised my children. When is this woman going to have something to say that applies to my life?*

Well, I do have something to say to you (and to me, too, as a grandmother of five). Only it's not from me—it's from God. In the Bible God has a word of wisdom for women like you and me. He commands us, as "the older women" in the church, to teach and "admonish the young women to…love their children" (Titus 2:3-4).

Dear older, wiser, more experienced mother, work out God's Word to you by passing on what you know about raising children! You'll be a hero…and a lifesaver too! Plus you'll be fulfilling God's calling on *your* life!

More Wisdom Regarding ...
My Children

And these words which I command you today
shall be in your heart.
You shall teach them diligently to your children,
and shall talk of them
when you sit in your house, when you walk by the way,
when you lie down, and when you rise up.
Deuteronomy 6:6-7

Train up a child in the way he should go,
and when he is old he will not depart from it.
Proverbs 22:6

My son, give me your heart,
and let your eyes observe my ways.
Proverbs 23:26

Do not provoke your children,
lest they become discouraged.
Colossians 3:21

Continue in the things which you have learned
and been assured of, knowing...that from childhood
you have known the Holy Scriptures,
which are able to make you wise for salvation
through faith which is in Christ Jesus.
2 Timothy 3:14-15

There is no nobler career
than that of motherhood at its best....
There is no higher height to which humanity can attain
than that occupied by a
converted, heaven-inspired, praying mother.[1]
—*Elisabeth Elliot*

I Need More Help with...
My Children

A promise is a promise! And I promised you "Ten Timeless Principles for Childraising." So here are the rest of them. Whisper a prayer as we proceed to add to our list of guidelines for godly mothering that already includes teaching, training, instructing, and correcting our children.

5. *Cherish them*—From beginning to end, the book of Proverbs shows us this tender quality that resides in the heart of a godly mother toward her sons and daughters. For instance,

- ♪ Solomon, the writer of most of the Proverbs, described himself as well-loved, his mother's darling, an object of her tender loving care, as "tender and the only one in the sight of my mother" (Proverbs 4:3).

- ♪ The mother in Proverbs 31:2 emoted, "What, my son? And what, son of my womb? And what, son of my vows?" Not only does this cherished son matter to his mother, but he matters so much that she has vowed him to God.[2] Her words tumble forth, with each additional phrase adding to the intensity of her emotion.[3] Her child (personally) is a child from her own body (physically) and has been dedicated to God (spiritually).

❧ In 1 Samuel 1 we meet Hannah, who wanted a child so badly she wept and could not eat (verse 7). She declared to God in agonizing prayer, "If You will…give your maidservant a male child, then I will give him to the LORD all the days of his life" (verse 11).

Two things seem to call out to mothers from these scriptures. From the *child's* perspective, each one must know in his own heart of his special place in his mother's heart. If you're a mom, dear one, does each of your children know that he or she is cherished, well-loved, precious to you? And from the *mother's* perspective, each of your children must be dedicated to God, to use as He wills, to send where He wills. Has your love grown to become the greatest love of all, a love that dedicates your cherished ones to God?

6. *Take care of them*—You might be surprised (even shocked) to learn how many Christian moms are lax in this all-important area of TLC, tender loving care. But daily care for your children is definitely one of God's principles of wisdom for His mothers. Plus it's another way that we follow God's pattern of love. God feeds us as His children, clothes us, gives us what we need to drink, and gives us rest (Matthew 6:25-32 and 11:28)…and we should do the same for our children. Also, a look at the daily life of God's ideal woman—and mom!—in Proverbs 31 shows us that her daily tasks included providing and giving food to her household (verse 15) and seeing to their clothing needs (verse 21).

So now I ask you, where are you on this divine measuring scale for loving and taking care of your children? I know from firsthand experience that sometimes this is the last thing we want to think about in our busy, helter-skelter days! But as a wise-mom-in-the-making, I had to learn to turn things around. And I'm asking you to do the same. Instead of waiting until the last minute to think about meals and menus, do it first. As soon as you're up and have your senses, plan the day's meals. Then do as much of the preparation as possible early in the day. Do as God does, who not only knows what we need, but follows through and actually provides it! Make it a priority. That's what wise moms do.

(And just a little P.S.—to be *really* wise, plan your meals and make your grocery list for the entire week. I usually do this on Sunday afternoon, with my planner, grocery list, and recipe box in hand.)

7. *Pay attention to them*—Often it's hard to pay attention to our children. We're soooo busy! There is soooo much to do! And in some cases, there are soooo many children to take care of that somehow we fail to pay enough attention to them! And it's also true that if we don't pay enough attention to them, they will somehow, someway, at some time, let us know it!

But Proverbs points out that we need to consciously pay attention to our children's development and to their friends. Why? Because the tell-tale behaviors that signal to the wise parent exactly what is going on in her child's heart are right in front of her nose. All she has to do is pay attention to them! Learn from these proverbs:

> "Even a child is known by his deeds, by whether what he does is pure and right" (20:11). There are no surprises in the character development of our children...if we are paying attention! The basic nature of a person reveals itself early in life. Therefore, open your eyes, mom! What's he or she up to?

> "Be diligent to know the state of your flocks, and attend to your herds" (27:23). Like the care and

diligence of a good shepherd, we moms should be even more diligent in our watchcare over our sheep, our flock, our children.

"Whoever keeps the law is a discerning son, but a companion of gluttons shames his father" (28:7). Who are your children's best friends? Others who obey God's law...or fools and "good-for-nothings" (other translations of *gluttons*)? A wise mom pays close attention to the kinds of friends her child runs with!

"The rod and reproof give wisdom, but a child left to himself brings shame to his mother" (29:15). The standard interpretation of this proverb teaches that children who grow up with discipline become wise, while children who are left to themselves to do as they like or to figure things out for themselves are doomed to be unwise, undisciplined adults. Wise moms seek the opposite result: "Correct your [child] and he will give you rest; yes, he will give delight to your soul" (29:17).

8. *Promote peace in your home*—Here's a great childraising principle that bailed me out of many a squabble between my two girls. It takes some doing, but the peace is worth it. I call these "The Three C's" for peace in the home—Cast, Correct, and Cast (again).

"*C-asting lots* causes contentions to cease, and keeps the mighty apart" (Proverbs 18:18). In the days of Proverbs, casting lots was one way of determining God's will and settling matters between parties.

Today, in any family, moms often have to settle matters between brothers and sisters. In our household I applied the principle of casting lots through the age-old practice of drawing straws. For instance, is there an unpleasant work chore that someone must do? Or is one bowl of ice cream a wee bit larger than the others? Are the clamors of family members rising as they express what they believe to be right or fair? When you cast lots or draw straws, everyone has a fair chance and contention ceases as family members admit that it is a fair method of decision making. *Your reward* is a peaceful settlement between siblings who just might otherwise resort to force (or at least to forceful yelling!).

"**C-orrect** your [child], and he will give you rest; yes, he will give delight to your soul" (Proverbs 29:17). In other words, a child who is disciplined properly will bring joy and rest to your heart instead of anxiety and heartache. If tension is mounting in your home, it's usually a sure sign that someone needs to be disciplined in some way. Your home should be a place of peace. So correct your child and enjoy the peace and quiet and rest that results.

"**C-ast out** the scoffer, and contention will leave; yes, strife and reproach will cease" (Proverbs 22:10). Is one of the little ones arguing? Pushing? Picking a fight? Are the sounds of strife rising? Send (or cast out!) the instigator to his or her room for an attitude adjustment. Or sit him or her down in what I called "the waiting chair" for five minutes. While she is waiting (and, of course, being excluded from family fun!) she can calm down. And, if five minutes doesn't do it, up the count on the next round. (And don't forget that a wise mother uses her timer for a multitude of functions in childraising!)

9. *Require respect from them*—Home is the training ground for life. Whatever you desire from your children in their attitudes and actions, start instilling in them at home. And respect is foundational. Teaching your children to respect (honor) you and your position of authority as their parent means they will listen and learn from you. When a child respects his parents, he will respect all authority, whether at school, or later as a grown-up respecting his or her boss and governmental laws in general. And remember, this is the fifth of the Ten Commandments (Exodus 20:12)! If a child honors and respects authority, starting with his parents, he will honor all authority and his life will be blessed.

10. *Be patient with them*—"The fruit of the Spirit is...patience" (Galatians 5:22 NASB)...and that's what every mom needs 24/7! You can exhibit patience yourself in these ways:

- Give a soft answer (Proverbs 15:1).

- Study how to answer before you speak (Proverbs 15:28).

- Play-act.

What do I mean by play-act? Here's a typical scene. When my daughters were underfoot day-in, day-out and tension mounted, I used to ask myself, *Now how would a patient mother sound? How would a patient mother act? What would a patient mother say? What would a patient mother do?* Once I stopped and asked questions like these, I would then play-act. I would do what the Proverbs above said to do. I would speak to my girls in a tone of voice I had heard other wiser (and more patient!) mothers use. I would choose the words and posture exhibited by moms I respected.

Just for Today...

Mothering is for life. And we've covered a lot of ground. (And I'm sure you'll agree there is a lot of ground we didn't cover!) But if you are a mom, that means you will be practicing these ten principles for childraising in varying degrees for a long time! So what can you do...just for today?

❑ Just for today...talk to the Lord about your children. Pour out your heart to Him. Share your concerns and inadequacies with Him. Ask Him for His help and wisdom. Purpose to be a mother who prays faithfully. Set up a prayer journal or pages for your children in your personal jounal. Never forget that "the effective, fervent prayer of a righteous [mother] avails much" (James 5:16)!

❑ Just for tomorrow...set up a time to talk to your husband about your children. Seek to establish standards for the family. Formulate and agree on a list of family standards. The list will change as your children grow and the issues of their lives shift, but there should always be a standard. Write out a few thoughts and share them with your husband. Be open to his thoughts and move forward together. Remember, "two are better than one" (Ecclesiastes 4:9)!

❑ Just for this week...talk to older and wiser Christian mothers who have gone before you. I've mentioned my corps of older women and advisors many times in this book. They were the biblical "older women" God put in my path just when I needed them. They did their part—they taught me how to love my children (Titus 2:3-4). And I did my part—I, as the "younger woman," sought them out and asked for help. Who will you turn to this week? And here's another question—What books will you begin reading this week that can help you with your needs as a mother?

Seeking a Heart of Wisdom

Everyone knows that actions speak louder than words. And somehow our children seem to especially know this. And because they live with us and witness firsthand our day-in, day out conduct, they will not listen to us preach something we don't practice. Therefore you and I must live out genuine faith before our children.

Our genuine faith accomplishes two things. First, it gives us credibility and a platform for teaching God's Word. But second, it gives our children a priceless model of a person who lives out a deep reverence for God and a dependence upon Him. If you want your children to love God and follow Him and His ways (and I know you do!), then you must let them see *you* love God and follow Him and His ways.

That's what Eunice and Lois did for their little Timothy (who became the closest companion and friend of the apostle Paul). This tag-team consisted of a godly mother and a godly grandmother. They had sincere faith, genuine faith, the real thing (2 Timothy 1:4-5).

Are you the real thing, Mom? If so, you live out these words written about Eunice, the mother of Timothy: "Timothy received…the gift of life twice from his mother. She gave him birth and then showed him what a life of faith could be."[4]

May this be true of you and me, dear one!

More Wisdom Regarding...
My Children

He maketh the barren woman to keep house,
and to be a joyful mother of children.
Praise ye the LORD.
Psalm 113:9[5]

Behold, children are a heritage from the LORD,
the fruit of the womb is His reward.
Psalm 127:3

But Jesus said,
"Let the little children come to Me, and do not forbid them;
for of such is the kingdom of heaven."
Matthew 19:14

Do not provoke your children to wrath,
but bring them up
in the training and admonition of the Lord.
Ephesians 6:4

The older women...[are to be]...teachers of good things—
that they admonish the young women
to love...their children.
Titus 2:3-4

God's Wisdom for...
Your Personal Life

The clothing of dignity stamps [God's woman]
with the Lord's acceptance,
as His faithful servant,
the child of His grace, and
the heir of His glory.[1]

13

I Need Help with...
My Appearance

ecently I overheard two Christian moms of preschoolers discussing a talk show they had both watched on television. The program had centered on women—even teenagers—who were obsessed with their appearance. In fact, they were living for the day they could afford (more specifically, charge on their credit cards!) plastic surgery and liposuction treatments to improve and enhance their looks. Now, the startling thing to me was not that the two women had watched the program. No, I was shocked that both of these women felt the same way about their looks and appearance as those interviewed on the TV program!

Unfortunately such views about beauty and thoughts of inferiority preoccupy the minds and hearts of many Christian women. But what does the Bible tell us about our appearance? What are God's timeless words of wisdom on this daily concern of beauty and appearance? What is His message to us?

Timeless Beauty Tips

#1. *True beauty is internal.* Throughout the Bible God focuses on what's inside, not on outward appearance. What is of utmost importance to God is your heart, dear one, not your face, your features, or your figure! So...what's inside? Let's look together at what God has done to make you beautiful in *His* eyes.

—You have been *transformed* by God on the inside. Where you were once "dead" in your trespasses and sins, God has made you "alive" together with Christ (Ephesians 2:5). That means you are now "His workmanship, created in Christ Jesus" (verse 10). Talk about beauty!

—You are also *a new creation.* The Bible says that "if anyone is in Christ, he is a new creation; old things have passed away; behold, all things have become new. Now all things are of God" (2 Corinthians 5:17-18). Imagine...all the old things—the old standards, the old priorities, the old beliefs, the old loves, and the old value systems—are gone! "In Christ" and as "a new creation" we instead see all things (including the issue of our appearance and looks) with a new perspective. For the first time we see all of life as God sees it and begin to live for eternity, not for earthly things.

—You are *fearfully and wonderfully made.* God reports that you (yes, you!) are one of His "marvelous" works (Psalm 139:14).

As I said above, true beauty is internal. And the transformations considered here take place on the *inside.* God *in* us and at work *in* us causes us to be beautiful in Him on the inside. And, as two well-worn sayings remind us, "beauty is only skin deep" and "it's what's on the inside that counts!" So, rather than put down the way you look or resent your appearance, remember who you are in Christ.

I don't know how these assurances from God's Word affect you, but I can tell you that they have been lifesavers for me! So much so that they have eliminated all my concerns about "self"-image. My thinking now goes like this: *If God has transformed me from the inside out, caused me to become a new creation, and put His stamp of approval on my appearance, then who am I to find fault with His creation?* Whenever I read or remember that I am a new creation and that I am fearfully and wonderfully made (and I can't help but add in my heart "…*exactly* the way I am!"), then I must take the next obvious step and "praise" Him (Psalm 139:14)!

#2. *True beauty is enhanced by spiritual growth.* Here's an all-too-familiar fact about our appearance: We learn from 2 Corinthians 4:16 that "our *outward* man is perishing"—the physical body is in the process of decaying, a process that leads finally to physical death. That's the bad news!

However, the good news is that even as your body is declining, "the *inward* man is being renewed day by day" (also verse 16). In other words, your soul is constantly growing and maturing in Christlikeness as you consume yourself with "the things which are *not* seen" rather than with "the things which *are* seen" (verse 18). Being obsessed with that which is *eternal* instead of that which is *earthly* makes a difference…even in our appearance! How?

I'm sure you're familiar with lovely women who exude spiritual strength and beauty. They are flesh-and-blood pictures of the verse at the beginning of this chapter. "Strength and honor" are their "clothing" (Proverbs 31:25). You hardly notice what they look like because you're so caught up in something they convey. There's a definite aura about them. No, there's no halo. But there is an air, a charm, a sparkle, a glow. And somehow you know it comes from within. It's spiritual.

What you are witnessing is a beautiful inner life radiating outward. As one has termed it, it's the "beauty treatment" of godliness and deep spirituality that helps them—and us!—to become truly lovely. It's the beauty of "patience, kindness, and joy" along with "a gentle, modest, loving character [that] gives a light to the face that cannot be duplicated by the best cosmetics and jewelry in the world."[2]

Meet Rebekah

As we first meet Rebekah, she is described by God as "very beautiful to behold" (Genesis 24:16). Yet the servant of Abraham, who was sent to find a wife for Abraham's son Isaac, was attracted to something else in this gorgeous woman. He was drawn to her obvious compassion toward him as a tired man who had trekked hundreds of miles across the burning desert, to her sweet willingness to minister to him by bringing him water, and by her energy as she "hastened" and "ran" to tote enough water to refresh his ten camels! You see, this *servant* was not looking for a model. He was looking for a *model servant!* And that quality is found only on the inside, in the heart!

That's what we want—inner beauty! And a sure way for you and me to encourage our spiritual growth and to definitely (and dramatically!) enhance our inner beauty "day by day" (2 Corinthians 4:16) is by dipping into God's fountain of beauty—His Word, the Bible—day by day. So...let the beauty treatment begin!

#3. *True beauty is a matter of the heart.* We can't leave our beauty treatment without considering what I call "the queen of truths" for wise women. Here's how the apostle Peter put it:

> Do not let your beauty be that outward adorning
> of arranging the hair, of wearing gold, or of putting
> on fine apparel; but let it be the hidden person of
> the heart, with the incorruptible ornament of a
> gentle and quiet spirit, which is very precious in
> the sight of God (1 Peter 3:3-4).

Peter is not telling us to ignore attempts at a pleasing appearance. He is rather pointing the finger at those who are so obsessed with what's on the outside that they fail to take care of what's on the inside—the inner person of the heart. And how can we take care of the heart? By tending to a gentle and quiet spirit. By concentrating on godly character, which is "precious in the sight of God."

Unfortunately, it is true that "man looks at the outward appearance" (1 Samuel 16:7). This may not be right, and it may not be fair—but it is true. But here's another truth—"The LORD does not see as man sees...the LORD looks at the heart" (also verse 7). So make it a priority to tend to your heart, to your faith, and to your character. *This* finds favor with God. *This* is precious in His sight! So whatever amount of time you spend maintaining your physical looks, do even more to cultivate your inner character.

Checklist for Your Heart

We'll get to your actual outward clothing and appearance in the next chapter. But for now, we are interested in visiting God's spiritual clothing closet and putting on the apparel that is "very precious in the sight of God" (1 Peter 3:4). Look now into the mirror of His Word and check out your heart. How does your adornment match up with God's list for His best-dressed women?

- Put on...the new man (Ephesians 4:24).

- Put on...tender mercies,

❧ Put on...kindness,

❧ Put on...humbleness of mind,

❧ Put on...meekness, and

❧ Put on...longsuffering (Colossians 3:12).

❧ Put on...a gentle and quiet spirit (1 Peter 3:4).

❧ Put on...a cloak of humility (1 Peter 5:5).

Just for Today...

As I said before, many women worry about their appearance or don't like their looks. They fuss and fume over what they consider their lacks and shortcomings in the Beauty Department. If you are one of these women...or you know other women or have daughters who struggle in this area, please follow and share these steps to wisdom.

❑ Just for today...take the truths we've gone over in this chapter to heart. Believe it—*you* are God's workmanship! *You* are a new creation in Christ! *You* are fearfully and wonderfully made! *You* are one of God's marvelous works! So just for today follow David's example. As he thought upon truths like these, he exulted, "I will praise You" (Psalm 139:14)! Why not thank and praise Him now?

❑ Just for tomorrow...purpose to repeat the step above if (or when!) you find yourself complaining or displeased with your looks, or comparing your appearance with that of someone else, someone you consider to be more beautiful than you. Focus instead on the spiritual realities of who you are in Christ.

Also, just for tomorrow (and all your tomorrows!) seek to nurture your inner beauty. Look to God's Word. Spend time there, reading, meditating, praying. Then allow others to benefit from His transforming grace and the power of His Word. With God's help be as kind as you can be to as many people as you can. Be gracious. Be sweet. Be loving. Be an encourager. Be patient. Be gentle. Be compassionate. Be helpful.

That's what Rebekah did as she spotted an elderly, lone, tired, dusty traveler. As she poured out water, the evidence of her heart was obvious in its overflow. True beauty is a gift from God...and of God. As one pastor-of-old commented regarding Rebekah's beautiful spirit of servanthood, "To be my very best this very hour, to do the very best for those about me, and to spend this moment in a spirit of absolute consecration to God's glory...is in the noblest sense to live for eternity."[3] May such beauty be true of you and me today, tomorrow, and every day!

❏ Just for this week...do the same each day. Seek to multiply your one beautiful day times seven. Begin your beautiful strand of beautiful deeds by adding seven beautiful "pearls" to it this week. Dedicate your mind to thinking on what is true about yourself, about your core, about your heart, about what God has done for you (Philippians 4:8). Honor God by refusing to think otherwise. Then a wonderful thing will happen! You'll find that the more you think on the truths from God's Word about your internal beauty, the less you'll think about yourself...and the more you'll think about the Lord and others. What a marvelous day it will be when you don't even think about yourself!

Seeking a Heart of Wisdom

It has been my joy for many years to write extensively on what it means to be "A Woman After God's Own Heart."[4] And here we go again in yet another book! And, dear one, such a woman knows that beauty—true beauty—begins in the heart, inside a woman, at her very core. May the prayer of your heart be, "Lord, grant that I may become inwardly beautiful." The wise woman after God's own heart seeks to be noticed, not for her clothing, jewelry, figure, skin tone, or hairdo, but rather for her kind and good character. She follows God's timeless guidelines of being quiet and sensible in manner and being noticed for the "good works" that accompany a woman who professes godliness (1 Timothy 2:9-10).

Like God's ultimate woman after His own heart and like His ultimate woman of wisdom—the Proverbs 31 woman—may it be said of you and me that "strength and honor are her clothing" (Proverbs 31:25). May others say of us, "Strong and beautiful is her clothing of moral character and honorable conduct! She is a true woman of excellence!"

More Wisdom Regarding...
My Appearance

Before I formed you in the womb I knew you;
before you were born I sanctified you.
Jeremiah 1:5

God demonstrates His own love toward us,
in that while we were still sinners,
Christ died for us.
Romans 5:8

Blessed be the God and Father of our Lord Jesus Christ,
who has blessed us with every spiritual blessing....
He chose us in Him before the foundation of the world...
having predestined us to adoption as sons...
by which He has made us accepted in the Beloved.
Ephesians 1:3-6

For in Him dwells all the fullness of the Godhead bodily;
and you are complete in Him.
Colossians 2:9-10

Being confident of this very thing,
that He who has begun a good work in you
will complete it until the day of Jesus Christ.
Philippians 1:6

As we look up to Him, pray to Him, think on Him,
serve Him, worship Him, do all we do unto Him,
obey Him, and love Him
with all our hearts, souls, strength, and minds,
His beauty shines through our lowly efforts.
And then *He* is glorified!
—*Elizabeth George*

14

I Need More Help with...
My Appearance

As a young teenage girl in junior high school, I was required to take a home economics class on grooming. Now, *that* was a class none of us girls complained about! Oh no! We thrived on learning about the proper way to wash our faces, take care of our skin, apply makeup, groom our nails. We even learned tips on good posture, how to enter a room, how to "sit like a lady," and.... On and on the wonderful topics and beauty tips went. We couldn't get enough!

Every woman—whether younger or older—is concerned about her appearance. Some, as we learned in the previous chapter, are overly concerned. And I hope and pray you now realize that true beauty is what's inside.

More Timeless Beauty Tips

In the last chapter we began a list of God's timeless beauty tips. Now let's continue. To review what we've learned, true beauty is internal, true beauty is enhanced by spiritual growth, and true beauty is a matter of the heart.

But there is no getting around the fact that...

#4. *True beauty is also external.* I'm sure you agree by now that your appearance is a mirror of what's happening (or not happening!) on the inside. It's an outward reflection of the inner self (1 Peter 3:4). However, there's no doubt that you can do a few things to maintain and improve your external appearance. What are God's guidelines in this all-important area? Exactly what is His dress code?

Modesty—God says to "adorn" yourself in "modest apparel" (1 Timothy 2:9). This prescription for godly dress means wearing decent clothing that reveals a properly adorned chaste heart.[1] As one scholar comments, "respectable and honorable apparel reflects a godly woman's inner life."[2] Therefore modesty in a woman exhibits a right attitude of mind, because what a woman wears is, as I said, a mirror of her mind and heart. God desires all of His women to be "chaste" (Titus 2:5). Therefore, your appearance should be modest—it should show forth a chaste and pure heart.

As I thought about modesty, I turned to a common English dictionary for help. There I found that *modesty* is also defined simply as a lack of excesses or pretensions. Modesty is wrapped up in moderation and in decency mixed with decorum. So, to be modest, according to Mr. Webster, is to behave, dress, and speak in a way that is considered proper. (And I might add, proper before God!)

Propriety—God says to "adorn" yourself with all "propriety" or reverence (1 Timothy 2:9). *Propriety* refers to modesty mixed with humility.[3] Clearly this is a tall order and should be approached prayerfully and devoutly. I can never think about this calling to propriety and reverence in clothing without thinking of the wisdom of Proverbs 31:30, which says, "Charm is deceitful and beauty is vain, but a woman who fears the LORD, she shall be praised."

Moderation—God says to "adorn" yourself with "moderation" or with a serious air of self-restraint, "not with braided hair or gold or pearls or costly clothing" (1 Timothy 2:9). In the day of Paul and Timothy, women wore their wealth. They tended to dress excessively. For them, the "more" you saw revealed the "more" they possessed. Paul says, not so for the woman who is obsessed with holiness!

Dressing with *moderation* also refers to self-control "so as not to lead another into sin" (1 Timothy 2:9).[4] By contrast, the prostitute in Proverbs 7:10 wore "the attire of a harlot" or, in the words of another, she was "dressed to kill"![5]

I like what my former pastor, Dr. John MacArthur, wrote in his commentary on the appearance you and I are to desire as godly women:

What's a Woman to Wear?

How does a woman discern the sometimes fine line between proper dress and dressing to be the center of attention? The answer starts in the intent of the heart. A woman should examine her motives and goals for the way she dresses. Is her intent to show the grace and beauty of womanhood? Is it to show her love and devotion to her husband and his goodness to her? Is it to reveal a humble heart devoted to worshiping God? Or is it to call attention to herself, and flaunt her wealth and beauty? Or worse, to attempt to allure men sexually? A woman who focuses on worshiping God will consider carefully how she is dressed, because her heart will dictate her wardrobe and appearance.[6]

So what's a woman to wear? The next time you look in your mirror, check yourself out…

...for modesty—"Do I look pure?"

...for propriety—"Is my appearance reflecting a proper image of a woman of God?"

...for moderation—"Would my appearance cause someone to stumble?"

...for wisdom—The wise woman will pass this test!

And here's another test. We are not to "adorn" ourselves with too much (1 Timothy 2:9). So ask yourself the "too much" question—am I wearing too much? Too much makeup? Too much jewelry? Are my clothes too fancy? Too gaudy? Am I wearing items that would cause others to notice me and my clothing, hair, or jewelry, rather than my "godliness" and "good works" (verse 10)?

Practical Beauty Tips

It truly is what's on the inside that counts with God! However, there are a few additional practical steps we can take to represent Jesus Christ well so that what others see in us as Christian women will honor Him (Titus 2:5).

- Dress up—The Old Testament heroine, Queen Esther, chose to wear her royal robes into the presence of her husband, the king (Esther 5:1). The Proverbs 31 woman wore silk and purple (Proverbs 31:22). Each of these godly women dressed with a touch of class, wearing what was right for the occasion and proper in her day and time.

For years I've taught the following principles about "dressing up" to future pastors' wives and women in Christian leadership: "Become a role model for your peers and those you want to lead. And always model yourself after people you respect. Don't model yourself after the group in which you run.... Be different, if it means being cleaner, neater, and better groomed than the group. It is always better to arrive at any function looking slightly better than others rather than slightly worse than the others."[7]

Why not bless others with a pleasing appearance? Others will be most grateful! And you will be setting a good example.

🎵 Fix up—As I've often shared with women, you and I *can* make an effort to create a pleasing appearance. When I'm getting ready in the morning, I always think about my husband and about the fact that he has to look at me. What is it he sees? Something fresh (as in a freshly washed face, freshly fixed hair, and fresh makeup)? Something clean (as in wrinkle-free, spot-free, odor-free clothes)? Something bright (as in a bright smile, a little color here and there)? Even when my children were still living at home, I was always concerned that they be able to look at me, rather than needing to avert their eyes because of what I looked like! I wanted them to be proud of me when I picked them up from school or took them to a friend's house, piano lessons, or their church group.

So fix up...a little! Make up...a little! Dress up...a little! Shape up...a little! Again, others will be most grateful!

🎋 Clean up—We've all heard that cleanliness is next to godliness. Plus Proverbs teaches us that "ointment and perfume delight the heart" (27:9). Both are pleasant and heartwarming and indicate that someone has gone to the trouble to spruce up. Once again, others will be most grateful!

🎋 Look up—Back to the Lord we go! As we look up to Him, pray to Him, think on Him, serve Him, worship Him, do all unto Him, obey Him, love Him with all our hearts, souls, strength, and minds (Luke 10:27), and are consciously aware of His presence, *His* beauty shines through our lowly efforts. And then *He,* dear sister-in-Christ, is glorified (Matthew 5:16)! To Him be all blessing and glory and wisdom, thanksgiving and honor and power and might, forever and ever. Amen (Revelation 7:12)!

Just for Today...

One of the things I learned from my home economics class on basic grooming is that good grooming means daily grooming. That's how teeth are tended to, skin is cared for, hair is maintained, and nails are kept up. So, when it comes to your personal physical appearance...

❑ Just for today...follow these four steps: Fix up...a little! Make up...a little! Dress up...a little! Shape up...a little! Think about your family members and the people you see every day. Think of your efforts as blessing them, as giving them a gift.

And here's another thought: Think about the Lord as you prepare yourself to represent Him to the world. What impressions do you give to others about what Christians and Christianity are? When you take care of your appearance, God is represented in a good light.

❏ Just for tomorrow…remember, good grooming is done daily. So tomorrow set aside a small pocket of time, like 10 to 20 minutes, for taking care of your appearance. Most women love the "makeover" shows on television. The premise behind these makeovers is that if a woman will spend just 20 minutes each morning on her looks, it will set her apart from others (in a good way). We're not talking about wowing others. We're just talking about looking nice, pleasant, attractive, worthy of the Spirit of Christ who lives within you. And, as we've already noted, others will be most grateful!

❏ Just for this week…imagine (speaking of makeovers!) what one week of attention to your appearance will mean. If you think personal hygiene takes too long and you're already too busy, take heart. As you repeat your efforts, they will be accomplished more quickly. You'll automatically become more organized and streamlined as you develop a quick and simple daily routine of taking care of yourself.

And here's another piece of advice an older and wiser Titus 2–type woman gave me. Put a Scripture memory verse in your bathroom or on your makeup table. Then, as you tend to the "outward man" (2 Corinthians 4:16), you will also be adorning "the hidden person of the heart" (1 Peter 3:4). After all, all things are to be done for the Lord (Colossians 3:23).

Seeking a Heart of Wisdom

This is a lot to take in, isn't it? But our appearance is a daily thing. It's where we live. Every day of our lives we must go to our closets. We must fling open the closet doors, peer inside, think through our day, and select the clothes we put on. While we are not responsible for how we were born, for our physical genetics and features, we *are* responsible for what we choose to wear and not wear, for the message we choose to send through our dress and grooming.

So what does the wise woman do? How does the wise woman choose? What message does the wise woman seek to send forth?

In a nutshell, she seeks to send forth a loud and clear message that she belongs to God. That she has put God at the center of her life. That she is truly "all about God." Therefore she "adorns" (meaning arranges, makes ready, and puts in order) herself properly and piously and prayerfully for Him and in a way that honors Him and speaks well of Him. It is a calling to the purposeful, orderly, and proper arrangement of your appearance as a habitual way of life.

What is your habitual way of life, my friend? Where is your heart set? On impressing others...or on impressing God? On turning the eyes of others...or on catching the look of approval in God's eyes? On drawing attention to yourself...or on drawing attention to your godliness and good works so that your Father who is in heaven is glorified (Matthew 5:16)?

As I said before, the wise woman will pass this test.

More Wisdom Regarding... My Appearance

And there a woman met him,
with the attire of a harlot and a crafty heart.
She was loud and rebellious.
Proverbs 7:10-11

Strength and honor are her clothing.
Proverbs 31:25

Charm is deceitful and beauty is vain,
but a woman who fears the LORD,
she shall be praised.
Proverbs 31:30

In like manner also, that the women adorn themselves
in modest apparel, with propriety and moderation,
not with braided hair or gold or pearls or costly clothing,
but, which is proper for women professing godliness,
with good works.
1 Timothy 2:9-10

Beloved, do not imitate what is evil, but what is good.
3 John 11

Discipline is evident on every page of the life of
Daniel…. The first thing that sets Daniel apart
from…others is his decision [about what] not to eat….
It was the beginning of the Lord's preparation of a man
whose spiritual fiber would be rigorously tested later on.[1]
—*Elisabeth Elliot*

Are there things you desire to accomplish,
goals you'd like to achieve,
dreams you'd like to see come true
in the area of God's purposes?
Then you require the energy that following
God's wise principles regarding your eating habits
will bring to your life.
—*Elizabeth George*

15

I Need Help with...
My Appetite

"You are what you eat."

I'm sure you've heard this saying before...and so have I. I've also heard multiple arguments on whether this statement is true or not. But I'm sure you also agree that what you take in and feed on—whether physically, mentally, or visually—has a powerful effect on the quality of your daily life. It can also influence the direction your life takes. But let's focus specifically on physical appetite, what a woman eats.

I still remember (all too well!) a phase in my life when I tried to gain the energy I needed to fulfill God's will for me as a young wife and mother of preschoolers by drinking colas and eating candy, cookies, and (I confess!) even the cookie dough! And I also remember the extensive (and expensive!) glucose-drinking and blood work it required for a doctor to determine that I was taking in too much sugar—more than my body could process. This state was causing me to be a woman who was sluggish, drowsy, and needed a nap every day after lunch. For me the statement was true—I was what I was eating. I was a junk food addict. (Perhaps you can relate!)

Well, after this ordeal, believe me, I wanted to know what God had to say on the subject of food. After all, I was seeking to live for Him and to live out His purposes for me. Yet it was obvious that the plan I was following was failing. I was on the wrong track, a track that was clearly leading to an unhealthy lifestyle and sabotaging my dreams of a life of energy, order, and achievement on the homefront and in my personal life. I was unwisely looking in the wrong places for the energy I wanted—and oh-so-desperately needed!—as one of God's busy women.

So back to the Bible I went, looking for God's wisdom on this daily issue of diet in a busy woman's life. And, of course, there it was...right in my Bible—God's timeless principles for what a wise woman eats and does not eat.

Do you want more energy? Or should I say, do you *need* more energy? Are there things you desire to accomplish, goals you'd like to achieve, dreams you'd like to see come true in the area of God's purposes? Then follow God's guidelines regarding your eating habits. Doing so will bring the much-needed energy to your life. Here now are a few practical principles that could be considered to be *the big ones!*

Better Eating...God's Way!

An amazing scripture puts a completely spiritual spin on our eating habits. It's this: "Therefore, whether you *eat* or *drink*, or whatever you do, do all to the glory of God" (1 Corinthians 10:31). This timeless truth says that it's possible for you and me to eat in a way that glorifies and honors our Lord. Just think about that for a second. You and I, two of God's women, can give glory to God in the everyday way we eat and drink. How? By following God's rules for better eating, rules like...

Rule #1—Do not eat too much. Why? One reason is obvious. We feel terrible when we've eaten in excess. We can actually feel sick. The Bible puts this feeling in very vivid terms—"Have you found honey? Eat only as much as you need, lest you be filled with it and vomit it" (Proverbs 25:16). (Now, that's vivid!)

But I found two other reasons in the Bible for not eating too much. One I had already experienced…and the other was a surprise, something I hadn't thought about before. According to Proverbs, God's book of wisdom, eating too much (called "gluttony" in the Bible) *costs too much* and *causes us to sleep too much*. As Solomon put it, "The drunkard and the glutton will come to poverty, and drowsiness will clothe a man with rags" (Proverbs 23:21). In other words, "there are two kinds of drunkards—those who drink too much and those who eat too much."[2]

> *First, the physical*—As I said, I knew from firsthand experience about the sleepy effect reported in this verse as a result of overeating. Drowsiness, laziness, and dullness are sure results from overeating and from eating the wrong kinds of food. Yes, I already knew all about living in a daze. And here I was reading in the Bible that those who overindulge in food will suffer physically. They will live in a fog, a tired state and a sort of drunken stupor. As a result they will lack the energy and clearheadedness needed to do their work and manage their lives that are busy and filled to the brim with responsibilities (Proverbs 23:20-21).
>
> *Next, the financial*—But here was the surprise for me—not only will one who overeats pay a price physically, but she will also pay a price financially. She will suffer from a lack of funds. As one scholar so succinctly dubbed this passage of Scripture, the unwise ones go "From Revelry to Rags"![3] We can almost imagine self-conversations like this: *Wow, it was fun while it lasted…but, boy-oh-boy, was there a price to pay!*

If you think about it, where does most of the food a woman eats come from? It comes from her efforts. She shops for it. She purchases it. She pays for it. She brings it home. Whether at a restaurant or a grocery store or a food warehouse, each woman puts out money for the food she puts into her mouth and into her pantry.

Now, an exercise—Think of all that you desire for your family and for yourself that involves finances. And think of all the people and concerns you could bless with your money. Do you want to get out of debt? Do you want to save for your children's or grandchildren's college years? Do you want to send your teen to your church's youth retreat? Do you desire to contribute to a worthy ministry cause? Do you want to pay off your home mortgage early? Maybe even take a much-needed vacation? Then you and I must think twice (and pray!) before we go out to eat or run to the food store. Money not spent on eating too much (or eating out too much, or stocking your cupboards with too much junk food) is money in the bank, money for better things than the sensual indulgence of overeating.

And, of course, the spiritual—As I researched this principle (frankly not liking what I was reading!), I found yet another principle for wise living, a principle in the area of the *spiritual* life. One commentator put it this way—"Bad habits grow together."[4] The implication is that overeating goes against the wisdom and teaching of God's Word...which leads to a life of guilt...which leads to a seared conscience...which leads to a deadening of the heart to spiritual truth. As you can see, overeating has far greater consequences than merely becoming overweight! It affects your spiritual life.

Plus, the practical—And what about your time and your life? Quite simply, the glutton's "*time* is divided between eating...and sleeping."[5] This misuse of time and life is the practical effect of a failure to manage your appetite God's way!

A prayer for wisdom—Lord, may a lifestyle of physical fatigue, financial folly, spiritual dead-

ening, and the practical misuse of time not be
true of me. Help me be a woman who yearns to
live my life in a wise way—in *Your* way.

Just for Today...

It's true that we learn wisdom from failure much more than
from success. And frankly, I know many women who have failed
in this area of appetite and are presently at work waging a battle
against their eating habits. I'm in their camp, and I heartily
applaud them. It's also true that habit is either the worst of mas-
ters or the best of servants. And bad habits reap failure for us in
the Food Department. So now we must begin...just for today...to
break the cords of harmful habits and replace them with a chain
of good habits so that God's strong spiritual disciplines become
the best of servants.

❏ Just for today...write out, memorize, and carry with you
1 Corinthians 10:31—"Therefore, whether you *eat* or
drink, or whatever you do, do all to the glory of God."
Seek to make this the rule of your eating and drinking
habits...just for today. Also pray the *Prayer for Wisdom,*
which I am repeating here. Pray it now and each time
you prepare to eat.

> "Lord, may a lifestyle of physical fatigue,
> financial folly, spiritual deadening, and the
> practical misuse of time not be true of me.
> Help me be a woman who yearns to live my
> life in a wise way—in *Your* way."

❏ Just for tomorrow...begin following this checklist as you
apply God's Rule #1—*Do not eat too much.*

   ❧   Eat only when you are hungry.

   ❧   Eat only after you pray.

• Eat only one helping.

• Eat half-portions.

• Eat on a small plate.

• Eat on a schedule.

• Eat what is healthy.

• Eat what will give you energy.

• Eat to the glory of God.

❏ Just for this week…keep records of your eating habits. I've learned the habit of journaling, and I recommend the same for you. Just for this week, write out 1 Corinthians 10:31 each day in a journal or a notebook. At the beginning of each day, write down your weight. Throughout each day, write down everything you eat and the exact time you eat it. Go a step further and record how you felt physically and mentally after you ate. Pay attention to what foods eaten in what quantities at what times put you down or picked you up in the Energy Department. Then you can make changes each day so that you become the vibrant Christian woman you desire to be.

Seeking a Heart of Wisdom

What is wisdom, after all? Here's one definition: Wisdom is "the ability to see with discernment….to view life as God perceives it."[6] Dear reader, God has spoken on our eating habits! He has given us *His* view, *His* wisdom, and *His* instruction. In short, He says *Do not eat too much.* Now, the question is, will we heed His wisdom? Will we take His wisdom to heart? Will we follow it? Will we make His principle ours? Remember, a wise woman seeks a heart of wisdom! And that wisdom includes how (and what and how much) we eat!

More Wisdom Regarding ...
My Appetite

A slothful man buries his hand in the bowl,
and will not so much as bring it to his mouth again.
Proverbs 19:24

When you sit down to eat with a ruler,
consider carefully what is before you;
and put a knife to your throat
if you are a man given to appetite.
Proverbs 23:1-2

All things are lawful for me, but all things are not helpful.
All things are lawful for me,
but I will not be brought under the power of any.
1 Corinthians 6:12

Whatever you do in word or deed,
do all in the name of the Lord Jesus,
giving thanks to God the Father through Him.
Colossians 3:17

Put on the Lord Jesus Christ,
and make no provision for the flesh, to fulfill its lusts.
Romans 13:14

$\mathcal{L}$et us not be Christians
as to the few great things of our lives,
and atheists as to the many small things
which fill up a far greater space of them.
God is in both,
waiting for the glory we can give Him in them.[1]
—*Dwight L. Moody*

I Need More Help with...
My Appetite

My daughter Courtney is a wonderful amateur chef. She is always trying to improve and add new skills and recipes to her mastery. She has even spent time in the classrooms of a famous Colorado cooking institute. So, quite naturally, Courtney's coffee table at home is usually spread with the cooking magazines she subscribes to. One of these publications is *Bon Appétit*...which translates into English as "good appetite" or "enjoy your meal"!

Well, my friend, most women enjoy their good and enjoyable eating a little too much! That's why we are looking to God for His timeless principles in the Eating Department. So far we have learned *Rule #1—Do not eat too much.* Now for...

Rule #2—Do eat only what is sufficient. I love this prayer from the Bible—"Feed me with the food You prescribe for me; lest I be full and deny You" (Proverbs 30:8-9). Other translations explain these verses to mean, feed me with the food that is *needful* and *sufficient* for me, *just enough* to satisfy my needs.[2] One scholar actually put the prayer in these fairly familiar words—"Give me only my daily bread"—pointing out a distinction between human wants and human needs.[3]

And why is consuming only what is sufficient so important? Answer: so you and I are not tempted to forget or deny God or become independent of Him because we've overindulged. So we don't fail to trust in the Lord as our Provider. Obviously both are circumstances that endanger character! Those who have too much (and eat too much) are puffed up by the pride of prosperity, and those who have too little are tempted to mistakenly and bitterly assault God's mercy, righteousness, and justice.

Thus God's answer is eat…"just enough."

Rule #3—Do eat only what you need. This may sound like a repeat of Rule #2. However it contains an additional flavor, if you will. Instead of overindulging, God's wisdom for eating calls you and me to "eat only as much as you need" (Proverbs 25:16). So, to deter us from sin, God says once again that we are simply to eat what is enough. In the wise words of Benjamin Franklin, eat to live, and do not live to eat.

Rule #4—Do not be mastered by anything. And note—"anything" includes food! In the New Testament we read these words of wisdom from the apostle Paul: "All things are lawful for me, but all things are not helpful. All things are lawful for me, but I will not be brought under the power of any" (1 Corinthians 6:12). Generally speaking, Paul is saying that not everything a Christian *could* do is helpful or beneficial or profitable or useful. Therefore, he or she doesn't do them!

To top off his argument on *helpfulness,* Paul adds the argument of *enslavement,* declaring "I will not be brought under the power of any." In other words, Paul is putting his foot down and refusing to become enslaved to or to be brought under the power of *anything!* Regardless of what *others may do,* and regardless of what *he could do,* Paul will not follow the crowd. He simply will not become a slave! Paul plays with the words of this principle:

> *All things* are in my *power*, but
> I will not be brought under the *power* of
> any of the *all* things.[4]

We know that sin is powerful and enslaving. Nevertheless, as women on the path to greater wisdom, we "must never allow sin to have...control, but must master it in the Lord's strength."[5] God can help us to master anything, even our appetite for food.

Rule #5—Do eat in a way that glorifies God. We've already looked at God's final word on all our behavior, including our eating—"Therefore, whether you eat or drink, or whatever you do, do all to the glory of God" (1 Corinthians 10:31). This means that even the most common acts of eating and drinking can be done in a way that honors our Lord. Imagine! We can actually eat in a way that brings honor and glory to God! Let's agree to give God glory and to honor Him when we eat, by *what* we eat, and *how* we eat. And a major side benefit will be thrown in as we follow this scriptural command—the caliber of our lives, as well as our worship, will improve. Preacher-of-old D. L. Moody wrote these words in the margin of his Bible beside 1 Corinthians 10:31—

> Let us not be Christians as to the few great things of our lives, and atheists as to the many small things which fill up a far greater space of them. God is in both, waiting for the glory we can give Him in them.[6]

Just for Today...

Hopefully by now your chain of good habits in this most needful area of the very food you put into your mouth is lengthening and strengthening. And hopefully by now you are realizing that your chain of good habits is created one habit at a time, one day at a time, and one week at a time. So...

❑ Just for today...seek to comprehend the five rules from God's Word considered in these two chapters:

> *Rule #1—Do not eat too much.*
>
> *Rule #2—Do eat only what is sufficient.*
>
> *Rule #3—Do eat only what you need.*
>
> *Rule #4—Do not be mastered by anything.*
>
> *Rule #5—Do eat in a way that glorifies God.*

Look again at each rule. Pinpoint the one that needs the most attention. What will you do about it...just for today? *Habit is overcome by habit.* That means old habits are overcome by new habits. Bad habits are overcome by good habits. So what new habit will you begin to groom to replace and overcome the one you selected, a habit that is not-so-wise?

❑ Just for tomorrow...look again at the checklist from the previous chapter for following God's guideline of eating "just enough." Now that we have four new rules to draw from, let's add to the checklist:

- Eat with God in mind.

- Eat to live instead of living to eat.

- Eat for health.

- Eat for energy.

- Eat with self-mastery.

- Eat as a Christian, not as an atheist.

❑ Just for this week...purpose, with God's help, to make it through one day at a time for one week. Imagine! If one day of God-honoring, God-glorifying eating practices is as a golden link in your chain of good habits, a week is an outstanding beginning for a life of wisdom! Purpose to add a link a day...for life.

Seeking a Heart of Wisdom

Honestly, I have to admit that I dislike writing on this subject. Why? Because I fear sounding "legalistic" or giving the impression that I have my act together in this area. Plus I know it's a difficult area for most women to "stomach." We simply don't want to hear about sensible eating (again!) and self-control (again!). And we don't want to have to think about them (again!). And we certainly dislike dealing with them!

But...at the same time, I want wisdom for my life! I desperately desire to be a wise woman, a woman who lives her life in a wise way. There are sooo many things I passionately long to do in my life and with my life and for the others in my life. Believe me, there is an urgency to live out God's will that arrives with each new sunrise! And I've decided that I don't want the remaining years, months, weeks, days, hours, and minutes of my life (and only God knows how many are left!) to be spent in a fog with a headache and a tired, overindulged body that can't pull off the desires of my heart. I just can't afford it! And I don't think you can either.

So, although it is hard to do, I do want to share the wisdom I've found in the Bible with the many, many women who write to me or share about their personal battles with weight gain and with numerous eating disorders. I know what a challenge managing the appetite is. But I also know that it is an assignment from God to me and to you. God calls us to "self-control" (Galatians 5:23), to "moderation" (1 Timothy 2:9), to "temperance" (1 Timothy 3:11), to "walk worthily" (Ephesians 4:1), to "walk in wisdom" (Colossians 4:5), and to "receive" and "apply" His timeless principles (Proverbs 2:1-2), even in the area of the food we choose to put into our mouths.

As we finish up this issue of appetite, food, and eating habits, I think you'll find the story on the next page to be absolutely delightful. It's a fitting (and fun!) illustration of many of the timeless principles of wisdom we've been sharing about this important area of a woman's life. Bon appétit! Enjoy!

Too Much of a Good Thing

Some friends of ours have eight children, and they all love ice cream. On a hot summer day, one of the younger ones declared that she wished they could eat nothing but ice cream! The others chimed agreement, and to their surprise the father said, "All right. Tomorrow you can have all the ice cream you want—nothing but ice cream!" The children squealed with delight, and could hardly contain themselves until the next day. They came trooping down to breakfast shouting their orders for choco-late, strawberry, or vanilla ice cream—soup bowls full! Mid-morning snack—ice cream again. Lunch—ice cream, this time slightly smaller portions. When they came in for mid-afternoon snack, their mother was just taking some fresh muffins out of the oven, and the aroma wafted through the whole house.

"Oh goody!" said little Teddy. "Fresh muffins—my favorite!" He made a move for the jam cupboard, but his mother stopped him.

"Don't you remember? It's ice cream day—nothing but ice cream."

"Oh yeah…"

"Want to sit up for a bowl?"

"No thanks. Just give me a one-dip cone."

By suppertime the enthusiasm for an all-ice-cream diet had waned considerably. As they sat staring at fresh bowls of ice cream, Mary—whose suggestion had started this whole adventure—looked up at her daddy and said, "Couldn't we just trade in this ice cream for a crust of bread?"[7]

More Wisdom Regarding...
My Appetite

For the kingdom of God is not food and drink,
but righteousness and peace and joy
in the Holy Spirit.
Romans 14:17

Do you not know that your body is
the temple of the Holy Spirit...?
Therefore glorify God in your body.
1 Corinthians 6:19-20

All things are lawful for me,
but all things are not helpful;
All things are lawful for me,
but all things do not edify.
1 Corinthians 10:23

Therefore, whether you eat or drink,
or whatever you do,
do all to the glory of God.
1 Corinthians 10:31

But the fruit of the Spirit is...self-control.
Galatians 5:22-23

The person who does not avoid small faults,
little by little slips into greater ones.
You will always be glad at evening
if you have spent the day well.
Watch over yourself, rouse yourself,
chide yourself, and no matter what others may do,
do not neglect yourself.
—*Thomas à Kempis*

The more self-disciplined you are,
the more you will progress.[1]
—*Thomas à Kempis*

I Need Help with...
Discipline

I admit that I need help with discipline…every day of my life! From my first decision each morning in answer to the sound of my alarm clock (will I respond or not? will I get up or snooze in?) to the final decision at day's end of putting my head on my pillow (will I read a little longer, work a little longer, watch television a little longer, or will I turn out the light and get to sleep so I can get up when the alarm goes off?), I need discipline.

No one has to tell you or me that discipline in every area of life is extremely important. You already know that discipline is important for what it produces in *you*—spiritual growth, personal accomplishment, and physical well-being. But discipline is also important for what it produces in you that is seen by *others* and in turn can produce in them—a motivating model and an example. Whether you like it or not, others are watching you. Your life has a positive or negative effect on everyone you live with, know, or encounter.

And yet, no matter how disciplined (or undisciplined!) you already are, there is always room for growth. There is always another area that you can tackle and improve. There is always something to learn, try, and perfect. So let's rethink and revisit this most important ingredient in the life of every wise woman. Let's continue to consider *why* a disciplined life is so critical. And most important, let's review what God has to say about discipline.

God's Wisdom Regarding Discipline

Recognize that discipline is a spiritual issue—Self-control and self-discipline are manifestations of God's Spirit working in our lives (Galatians 5:22-23). The Bible says that if we are walking by the Spirit (verse 16), if we are desiring and seeking to live our lives God's way, we will exhibit "self-control." This word literally means to be master of one's self. Picture wrapping your arms around yourself and grasping onto yourself and holding yourself in restraint. That's self-control! Try that the next time you have a desire to overindulge in some area. And remember… *character does not reach its best until it is controlled, harnessed, and disciplined.*

Readily acknowledge sin—It helps to understand that self-control is energized by the power of the Holy Spirit living in you. As you walk by the Spirit, He gives you the ability to overcome the temptations of the flesh (Galatians 5:16). But sin and disobedience "grieve" the Holy Spirit of God and "quench" the Spirit and His power to assist you in your fight against sin (Ephesians 4:30 and 1 Thessalonians 5:19). So, do you want to experience self-discipline? Then keep a short account with God. Quickly confess your sins (1 John 1:9), any of them and all of them. And the result? You will enjoy the power and beauty of a victorious life of Christian discipline.

Realize that discipline is an act of the will—Yes, self-control is a fruit of the Spirit, but God's Spirit will not force you to live spiritually. No, you must decide if you will or won't obey the Spirit's promptings in your life. The Holy Spirit doesn't lock your jaw every time you sit down to eat! And He doesn't automatically seal your mouth so that you don't yell at your children. The Spirit of God prompts, moves, impresses, and convicts you of error (John 16:8), but He will not force you to live a godly life. Instead He gently leads you as you read, study, pray, and seek to apply God's Word to every area of your life.

For instance, here are just a few issues in your life where God's wisdom of self-control and discipline are needed...and available:

> Your temper—*Whoever has no rule over his own spirit is like a city broken down, without walls* (Proverbs 25:28).

> Your mouth—*Even a fool is counted wise when he holds his peace; when he shuts his lips, he is considered perceptive* (Proverbs 17:28).

> Your eating—*Put a knife to your throat if you are a man given to appetite* (Proverbs 23:2).

> Your diligence—*Do not love sleep, lest you come to poverty; open your eyes, and you will be satisfied with bread* (Proverbs 20:13).

In each of these problem areas (as in all others!) you must decide how you are going to respond to that issue in your life. God's Spirit lives in you as a believer in Christ and is ready, willing, and able to assist you with your discipline.

Rejoice with each victory—The battle of the flesh is an ongoing and relentless one. However, as you (and I!) recognize that self-control is a spiritual issue, realize when and where self-control is needed, and then readily acknowledge your sin, God works in marvelous ways to bring about victory in your life. You *can* live a disciplined life! You *can* have self-control! You *can* manifest God's fruit of self-control for all to see as you follow Him. So celebrate with each win in your battle against temptation. Exult with the apostle Paul, who proclaimed, "but thanks be to God, who gives us the victory through our Lord Jesus Christ" (1 Corinthians 15:57). Thank God that there can be victory. And thank God for each and every victory, no matter how great or how small. Each victory is a stair-step toward a disciplined life.

Remember that discipline mirrors maturity—As you are able to win (with God's help!) the victories of self-control—one issue and one area at a time—an amazing thing begins to happen. You grow in spiritual maturity. As you exercise discipline and self-control in any area, your spiritual muscles begin to take shape and are strengthened and developed. You are then better able to handle that area the next time it comes along. It's as one gentleman observed—"No life ever grows great until it is focused, dedicated, and disciplined."

But a word of caution...growth in personal discipline and self-control is not static. You must constantly be about the process of exercising self-control. So stay on your toes!

God's Wisdom Requires Discipline

Speaking of staying on your toes, whenever I think of discipline—and the lack thereof(!)—my mind runs simultaneously to two women in the Bible. One gives us a negative example of self-mastery and control, and the other a positive one. One was lax and spiritually lazy, and the other stayed on her toes. With which one do you identify?

Meet Eve

Eve was the first woman on earth and the first woman to fail in the Discipline Department. When it came to the temptation to sin, she was weak, willful, and wanted too much. When the serpent began to interact with Eve, she readily entered into a dialog with the master deceiver, "a liar and the father of lies" (John 8:44, NASB). Eve basically…

…wanted too much,

…ate what was forbidden,

…talked too much, and

…held back too little.

Eve chose to disobey God's specific instructions. She also failed to seek counsel, to wait, to weigh her options, and to trust God. Instead Eve talked on and on with the devil himself, doubted God's wisdom, slipped into discontent, questioned God's goodness, lusted for more, ate the forbidden fruit, and also caused her husband to do the same.

Rather than walk the path of wisdom, Eve rushed headlong into foolishness on every front. Rather than being wise, Eve was a fool. Eve lived out this bit of biblical wisdom—"He who trusts in his own heart is a fool, but whoever walks wisely will be delivered" (Proverbs 28:26). Her foolish, sinful, selfish, and willful act plunged mankind forever into a fallen state.

Now Meet Abigail

What an amazing woman! Abigail is a woman who did things right and models godly discipline and self-control for every woman. At a time when everyone around her was out of control, our dear Abigail was quickly and quietly making sure everything was under control. In the biblical account of this woman's life, we see her (once again!) responding with great wisdom and self-control when her husband made a foolish decision that endangered many lives. Abigail acted with wisdom and self-control, stepped into the line of fire, defused the anger of the warrior David, and diverted a life-threatening situation and a potential bloodbath (see 1 Samuel 25). Abigail saved the day and the lives of all!

In this book we have been attempting to see God's wisdom applied to our every need. And do we ever need wisdom in the areas of self-control and discipline! Eve certainly needed it, Abigail needed it, you need it, and so do I! In every area of life God's wisdom involves exercising discipline, moderation, and self-control. As you can tell, discipline and wisdom are essential for godly living.

Just for Today...

How do you and I become disciplined women? One day at a time. And how do we cultivate lives marked by wisdom? By practicing God's timeless principles of wisdom one day at a time, one act at a time, as we master the art of self-discipline. Now, for that one day at a time...

❏ Just for today...pray for God's discernment to recognize and avoid your "little" faults for this day only. If your little faults are not avoided or dealt with today, you can be sure they will grow in power and be harder to deal with tomorrow! Long-lasting change begins with the tiniest increment of one decision made consistently day after day. So focus your attention...just for today...on one habit, weakness, excuse, or area of neglect. Look to the Lord for His strength. Look to God's Word for His wisdom. Discipline yourself to forsake your "little" faults. And don't forget to thank God for each "little" victory! Believe me, little will add up to much! You will soon discover that you are growing into a woman of great wisdom.

❏ Just for tomorrow...plan your day and pinpoint areas that need improvement. For instance, which area of your life needs God's help and control today? Name it...and then go to the Bible for verses that will help you overcome that area of neglect. Write the verses in your journal or notebook, or at least on 3" x 5" cards to carry with you. Also ask a friend to hold you accountable in the areas that need God's self-control. No victory is won without a battle. And your scriptures, journal, and accountability partner, coupled with your desire and the power of God's grace, are the weapons of your warfare. So use your arsenal! Gain the victory! Grow in wisdom!

❏ Just for this week...evaluate your growth in wisdom. A week is a long time, time enough to see marked progress. Time enough to notice measurable change. Time enough to "put away" what is ungodly and unwise, and replace it with more disciplined choices and conduct. Major progress and inroads can be made in a week of your life! Did you follow the wisdom presented in the verses you chose? Did you follow through on your accountability? Was it helpful? Rejoice in any progress. Then, without neglecting your new discipline, prayerfully choose the next area and begin the growth process all over again. And here's a warning—realize that any progress is for today only. Tomorrow and next week will require a fresh supply of the enabling power of the Holy Spirit.

Seeking a Heart of Wisdom

Does not wisdom cry out,
and understanding lift up her voice?
She takes her stand on the top of the high hill,
beside the way, where the paths meet.
She cries out by the gates, at the entry of the city.
Proverbs 8:1-3

My dear friend, as you reflect on the verses above, would you like to have wisdom and understanding? Would you like to stand in places of influence (places like your own home and community!) and give godly wisdom to all who would care to listen? Again, I know your answer—of course you would! Then you must embrace discipline as an essential and necessary element in your growth toward wisdom and maturity. Why? Because you cannot lead others—your children, your sisters-in-Christ, your friends, neighbors, and workmates—down a path of righteousness and discipline that you have not personally taken. Only as you exercise self-control will your life be a model for others to follow. With self-control as a guiding principle in your life, you, too, will be able to "cry out" and "lift up your voice." Others are watching your discipline and listening to your "voice." And they are glorifying God for you, for your life of discipline, and for your wisdom. So keep standing on that high hill for all to see and hear! Continue with discipline and you will continue to stand in the places of influence.

More Wisdom Regarding...
Discipline

He who is slow to anger is better that the mighty,
and he who rules his spirit than he who takes a city.
Proverbs 16:32

Whoever guards his mouth and tongue
keeps his soul from troubles.
Proverbs 21:23

Give me neither poverty nor riches—
feed me with the food You prescribe for me;
lest I be full and deny You,
and say, "Who is the LORD?"
Or lest I be poor and steal,
and profane the name of my God.
Proverbs 30:8-9

Giving all diligence, add to your faith virtue,
to virtue knowledge, to knowledge self-control.
2 Peter 1:5-6

I discipline my body and bring it into subjection,
lest, when I have preached to others,
I myself should become disqualified.
1 Corinthians 9:27

Resolutions for Life by Jonathan Edwards

*L*ive with all my might while I do live.
(He died at age 55.)

*N*ever lose one moment of time,
but improve it in the most profitable way possible.

18

I Need Help With...
Diligence

We've covered a lot, haven't we? Life, spiritual life, daily life, family life, and personal life. Obviously we haven't addressed our *every* need, but we've certainly considered some of the major areas and major needs of every woman's life. And I can think of no better way to end our book than with some words on diligence. Why?

Let me tell you a story…

One of my junior high school teachers still stands out as my all-time favorite educator. That's because Miss Spencer employed so many creative methods for teaching math. One learning device was a game she called "separating the sheep from the goats." Everyone began Miss Spencer's game by standing. Then, as the math drill progressed, each right answer allowed you to remain standing while one wrong answer meant you had to sit down. In the end, only the "sheep" were standing. The "goats" had been separated out.

Well, my dear woman-on-the-path-to-greater-wisdom, diligence is a definite mark of wisdom, for diligence truly separates the sheep from the goats in real life.

Or, as an almost-every-day example from my own life illustrates, diligence separates the "be's" from the "wanna-be's." Here's what happens. Just about every day I receive a letter, email, or phone call from someone who says, "I've always wanted to write a book. What advice can you give me?"

And my answer is always the same: "Write the book!"

Now, I know that there are many steps that go into getting a book published, but the first step and the main step and the ultimate step is (and always has been and always will be)…write the book! Until a book is written, that book is only a dream.

And what does it take to write a book…have an orderly house…get organized…graduate from college…find a job… provide clean clothes for your family…put meals on the table… study the Bible…keep your weight down and your body fit…homeschool your children…be a loving wife…serve in your church…put together a lesson to share some good things with someone else…or to do anything that is worthwhile?

Answer: It takes diligence! It takes work. It takes action. It takes staying with something until it is finished. And it takes diligence, work, action, and staying with something for millions of minutes, thousands of hours, hundreds of days, scores of weeks, months, and for as many years as God gives you and for as many years as the work—or the dream!—requires.

God's Wisdom Regarding Diligence

The book of Proverbs, called by many the "wisdom book of the Bible," was written some 3,000 years ago. And, would you believe it?—diligence is another major theme of this ancient book of wisdom. In Proverbs we learn that…

> ✤ Diligence affects our finances—"He who deals with a slack hand becomes poor, but the hand of the diligent makes one rich" (Proverbs 10:4).

- Diligence affects our livelihood—"He who tills his land will be satisfied with bread, but he who follows frivolity is devoid of understanding" (Proverbs 12:11).

- Diligence affects our income and productivity—"In all labor there is profit, but idle chatter leads only to poverty" (Proverbs 14:23).

- Diligence affects our contribution to society—"He who is slothful in his work is a brother to him who is a great destroyer" (Proverbs 18:9).

- Diligence affects our outcome—"Be diligent to know the state of your flocks, and attend to your herds; for riches are not forever" (Proverbs 27:23-24).

- Diligence affects our comfort—"He who tills his land will have plenty of bread, but he who follows frivolity will have poverty enough" (Proverbs 28:19).

- Diligence affects our households (Proverbs 31:10-31)—The wise woman…

    …rises while it is yet night (verse 15),

    …girds herself with strength (verse 17),

    …strengthens her arms (verse 17),

    …works into the night (verse 18), and

    …does not eat the bread of idleness (verse 27).

Therefore…

    …her husband has no lack of gain (verse 11),

    …she provides food for her household (verse 15),

...she makes tapestries for her home (verse 22), and

...her clothing is fine linen and purple (verse 22).

And then the reward...

...her children rise up and call her blessed
(verse 28),

...her husband also, and he praises her: "Many
daughters have done well, but you excel them
all" (verses 28-29).

Several Motivators for Diligence

If diligence accomplishes all of this (and more!) for you and
me, and if diligence is this important, then what can help us
become even more motivated in our diligence? Let's consider
these major contributors.

Awareness of the brevity of life—Many people choose to live
life in a waiting mode, with an "I'll get around to it" attitude or
an "I have all the time in the world" outlook. But the Bible
teaches us the opposite, that life is brief (Psalm 39:4-5). In fact,
God refers to our life as a vapor (James 4:14), as a breath (Job
7:7), as a shadow (1 Chronicles 29:15), as a blade of grass or a
flower that quickly withers away (1 Peter 1:24), and as passing
by swifter than a weaver's shuttle (Job 7:6).

Dear reading friend, there simply are no guarantees on the
length of your or my life! Our days are numbered, a number
that only God knows. Therefore we as women of wisdom must
live each day to the hilt! To the max! We must seize each and
every day! We must put the most into each day...and get the
most out of it. We must do as much as we can, love our families as much as we can, help as many people as we can, give as
much as we can in each precious 24-hour allotment of life. Each

part and parcel of each day, and each person in our every day—our marriages, our families, our homes, our ministries, our minutes, our work—must be relished and used wisely and fully...for it may be all we have!

Let your awareness of the brevity of life be a driving force. That's what the wise person does. And by contrast, fools squander, waste, and fritter away their time and their lives (Proverbs 18:9). Would you like to know how to waste a day? Just sleep in instead of getting up and getting going. Choose to sit or lie around instead of working (Proverbs 6:9). Everyone is tempted with laziness (1 Corinthians 10:13). That's the nature of our flesh. It's a "common" problem.

But the wise woman does not rest when she should be working. "Success" and accomplishment is a simple formula: The person who works for eight hours will accomplish twice as much as the one who works only four. And the person who labors for twelve hours will produce twice as much as the one who only works six. It's just as the Bible says—"In all labor there is profit" (Proverbs 14:23), no matter what that labor is! (And the flip side of this verse is also true—"Idle chatter leads only to poverty"!) So what will it be for you? The wise use of life, or the waste of life?

Awareness of the purpose of life—Understanding and grasping the truth about the purpose of your life is another catalyst to diligence. When you and I realize that we were made *by* God and *for* God, and that God has a purpose for each of our lives, we never live another day with "self" in mind. We instead begin living each day and each minute in each day for the Lord (Colossians 3:23). There's a new energy, a new direction, a new diligence. Why? Because there's a purpose!

Awareness of stewardship—With a sharp awareness of the brevity of life and the purpose of life, yet another contributor to diligence dawns on us—we begin to realize that each day and minute (and second!) of our lives is a gift from God. That means God intends us to manage our time and our lives for Him and to use them for His purposes. That means God expects each of us to be a steward of the life He entrusts us with. And what does the Bible say God requires of a steward? That he or she be faithful (1 Corinthians 4:2). One day every Christian will give an accounting to God for the use of his or her life (2 Corinthians 5:10). Therefore I seek to live each day with stewardship in mind for that one day. This mind-set certainly stimulates daily diligence in me!

Awareness of time—Or should I say, awareness of the time of day? I don't know about you, but I have peaks and valleys in my day. During my peak periods, I'm running on all cylinders. I'm moving at the speed of light! Things are happening! There's fire in my eyes and fervor in my steps.

But…during my valley times, when my energy is at a lower level, why, I can hardly get up out of my chair! I don't seem to have an ounce of energy left. I seem to be done, finished, kaput(!)…and it's only 2:00 P.M.! Do these two scenarios sound familiar?

Well, I've learned (through persistence and training, which equals discipline!) that during such down times you and I can still be productive and diligent by preparing for them (and, believe me, they *will* come!), by having a list of things we can do that take a lower level of energy. Things like…preparing tomorrow's menus…folding that pile of freshly-washed clothes… catching up on our daily Bible reading…working a Bible correspondence course (I completed a whole series of Bible courses while my children were taking their naps!).

So, diligence does not mean maintaining a frantic pace of life from start to finish. No, diligence just means pursuing a fruitful pace of life from start to finish as we purposefully move through the peaks and valleys, the ebb and flow, the springs, summers, and winters of our lives.

An Example of Diligence

When I think of diligence, I can't help but think of Ruth in the Old Testament.

Meet Ruth

Ruth had a hard life. She had lost her husband. She had left her country. And then she had to provide for her mother-in-law. If Ruth hadn't been diligent, she and her mother-in-law, Naomi, might have starved to death. Talk about motivation! But the real insight on Ruth's character (because that's what diligence is—a mark of character) comes from what was said about her attitude toward her responsibilities by another:

It has been fully reported to me, all that you have *done* for your mother-in-law since the death of your husband, and how you have left your father and your mother and the land of your birth, and have come to a people whom you did not know before. The LORD repay your *work* (Ruth 2:11-12).

Dear sister, our diligence should not be seen as a duty, but as a delight. Diligence comes from within and reveals our true character. May you and I follow in the footsteps of Ruth's diligence and trust the results to the Lord. For, as Ruth experienced, the Lord will repay your work and diligence.

Just for Today...

How do you and I become women of wisdom? (I've asked this question often!) I'm sure by this time you now know the answer...one day at a time. And again, How do we cultivate a life marked by wisdom? Through faithful diligence, practiced today...and extending into tomorrow...and continuing for a lifetime!

❑ Just for today...write out, memorize, and carry with you Colossians 3:23-24—"And whatever you do, do it heartily, as to the Lord and not to men, knowing that from the Lord you will receive the reward of the inheritance; for you serve the Lord Christ." Also ask yourself, "Since life is brief, how can I best spend this day?" Picture yourself as a steward. How will you answer to God for this day?

❑ Just for tomorrow...evaluate your peaks and valleys and plan for them. Keep thinking of your tomorrow with an eye to stewardship. How are you planning for its use? Design your day...by the minute! Then follow that blueprint...just for the day. Read the corresponding chapter of Proverbs for that day. You will more than likely find several verses dealing with diligence. Take note of them for your life and make note of them in your journal! Whatever you do, don't lose them!

❑ Just for this week...continue reading each day's chapter of Proverbs, noting all the verses of God's wisdom regarding this all-important area of diligence, work, industry, and perseverance. Continue planning for each day. At the end of your week, evaluate how you did and what corrections are needed next week. This is a process you'll want to repeat for the rest of your life! Why? Because it's a mark of wisdom.

Seeking a Heart of Wisdom

As we've already noted, the book of Proverbs has diligence as one of its major themes. It seems that a wise woman is a diligent woman. Her wisdom is seen in how she diligently handles her responsibilities today, and how she diligently prepares for tomorrow and for the rest of the life God has given her. She has taken the admonition of Moses to heart: "So teach us to number our days, that we may gain *a heart of wisdom*" (Psalm 90:12).

My dear heart-sister, we don't know the number of our days, but Moses speculated that "the days of our lives are seventy years; and if by reason of strength they are eighty years" (verse 10). According to Moses, we just might live to be 70 or 80.

So…let's do the math. How old are you today? Subtract that age from 70. What is the number? If God wills, that might be the number of years you have left to live a life of wisdom and diligence.

Now, at journey's end, we must leave one another to go about the business of putting God's timeless principles to work in our precious lives. But…just think what could be accomplished for God and for others if you and I were to seek a heart of wisdom and walk in diligence for our remaining years! Don't waste away your most important resource—your life! Number your days. And use each and every one of them for God's glory and the good of others. Be wise…seek wisdom…

for wisdom is better than rubies,
and all the things one may desire
cannot be compared with her.
Proverbs 8:11

More Wisdom Regarding...
Diligence

Go to the ant, you sluggard!
Consider her ways and be wise.
How long will you slumber, O sluggard?
When will you rise from your sleep?
Proverbs 6:6,9

Whatever your hand finds to do,
do it with your might.
Ecclesiastes 9:10

But as...you abound in everything—
in faith...in knowledge, in all diligence...
2 Corinthians 8:7

And let us not grow weary while doing good,
for in due season we shall reap if we do not lose heart.
Galatians 6:9

Be steadfast, immovable,
always abounding in the work of the Lord,
knowing that your labor is not in vain in the Lord.
1 Corinthians 15:58

⨍otes

Chapter 1—I Need Help with...Wisdom

1. Michael Kendrick and Daryl Lucas, eds., *365 Life Lessons from Bible People* (Wheaton, IL: Tyndale House Publishers, 1996), p. 140.

2. Charles Haddon Spurgeon.

3. Charles R. Swindoll, *The Tale of the Tardy Oxcart*, quoting from his book *The Strong Family* (Nashville, TN: Word Publishing, 1998), p. 613.

4. Ibid., quoting from his book *Living on the Ragged Edge*, p. 613.

5. M. R. De Haan and Henry G. Bosch, *Bread for Each Day* (Grand Rapids, MI: Zondervan Publishing House, 1980), April 16.

Chapter 2—I Need Help with...My Priorities

1. TLB.

2. Charles R. Swindoll, *The Tale of the Tardy Oxcart*, quoting Wayne Martindale, *The Quotable Lewis* (Nashville: Word Publishing, 1998), p. 468.

3. Ibid.

Chapter 4—I Need Help with...My Bible

1. Albert M. Wells, Jr., ed., *Inspiring Quotations—Contemporary & Classical* (Nashville: Thomas Nelson Publishers, 1988), p. 17.

2. Mark Porter, *The Time of Your Life* (Wheaton, IL: Victor Books, 1983), p. 114.

Chapter 5—I Need Help with...My Prayer Life

1. Charles Bridges, *A Modern Study of the Book of Proverbs*, revised by George F. Santa (Milford, MI: Mott Media, 1978), p. 17.

2. Eleanor L. Doan, *The Speaker's Sourcebook*, author unknown (Grand Rapids: Zondervan Publishing House, 1997), p. 196.

Chapter 6—I Need Help with...My Spiritual Growth

1. *Checklist for Life for Men*, quoting Jean-Nicolas Grou (Nashville, TN: Thomas Nelson Publishers, 2002), p. 183.

2. Thomas à Kempis, *The Imitation of Christ—Book 1* (Macon, GA: Mercer University Press, 1989), pp. 11-12.

3. Mark Porter, *The Time of Your Life* (Wheaton, IL: Victor Books, 1983), p. 114.

4. Sherwood Eliot Wirt and Kersten Beckstrom, *Topical Encyclopedia of Living Quotations*, quoting George B. Chisholm (Minneapolis: Bethany House Publishers, 1982), p. 152.

Chapter 7—I Need Help with...My Time

1. Author unknown.

2. Edward R. Dayton and Ted W. Engstrom, *Strategy for Living* (Glendale, CA: G/L Publications, 1978), p. 175.

3. Proverbs 31:10-31; Ephesians 5:22-24,33; 1 Timothy 2:9-15; Titus 2:3-5.

4. Elizabeth George, *A Woman After God's Own Heart*® (Eugene, OR: Harvest House Publishers, 1997).

5. Dayton and Engstrom, *Strategy for Living*, p. 180.

6. TLB.

Chapter 8—I Need Help with...My Schedule

1. Frank S. Mead, *12,000 Religious Quotations*, quoting W. Marshall Craig, gender changed (Grand Rapids, Baker Book House, 1989), p. 269.

2. Roy B. Zuck, *The Speaker's Quote Book*, adapted from *Gospel-Lite* (Grand Rapids: Kregel Publications, 1997), p. 126.

Chapter 9—I Need Help with...My Home

1. Eleanor L. Doan, *The Speaker's Sourcebook*, author unknown (Grand Rapids: Zondervan Publishing House, 1977), p. 267.

2. Elizabeth George, *God's Wisdom for Little Girls* (Eugene, OR: Harvest House Publishers, 2000).

3. Charles Bridges, *A Modern Study of the Book of Proverbs* revised by George F. Santa (Milford, MI: Mott Media, 1978), p. 527.

Chapter 10—I Need Help with...My Marriage

1. Marriage service from *The Book of Common Worship* (Philadelphia: Board of Christian Education of the Presbyterian Chruch, 1974).

Chapter 11—I Need Help with...My Children

1. Derek Kidner, *The Proverbs* (Downer's Grove, IL: InterVarsity Press, 1973), p. 147.

2. William MacDonald, *Enjoying the Proverbs* (Kansas City, KS: Walterick Publishers, 1982), p. 55.

3. Albert M. Wells, Jr., ed., *Inspiring Quotations—Contemporary & Classical*, p. 106.

Chapter 12—I Need More Help with...My Children

1. Elisabeth Elliot, *The Shaping of a Christian Family*, quoting an anonymous source (Nashville, TN: Thomas Nelson Publishers, 1991), pp. 95-96.

2. Kidner, *The Proverbs*, (Downer's Grove, IL: InterVarsity Press, 1973), p. 183.

3. Ibid. Proverbs 31:2 is an example of staircase parallelism, where each phrase repeats something from the prior phrase yet adds something new.

4. Michael Kendrick and Daryl Lucas, eds., *365 Life Lessons from Bible People,* (Wheaton, IL: Tyndale House Publishers, Inc.; 1996), p. 355.

5. KJV.

Chapter 13—I Need Help with...My Appearance

1. Charles Bridges, *A Modern Study of the Book of Proverbs*, revised by George F. Santa (Milford, MI: Mott Media, 1978), p. 738.

2. Neil S. Wilson, ed., *The Handbook of Bible Application* (Wheaton, IL: Tyndale House Publishers, 1992), pp. 56-57.

3. D. L. Moody, *Notes from My Bible and Thoughts from My Library* (Grand Rapids: Baker Book House, 1979), p. 19.

4. Elizabeth George, *A Woman After God's Own Heart*®, *A Young Woman After God's Own Heart*, and *A Woman After God's Own Heart*® Bible Study Series (Eugene, OR: Harvest House Publishers).

Chapter 14—I Need More Help with...My Appearance

1. John MacArthur, *The MacArthur Study Bible* (Nashville: Word Publishing, 1997), p. 1863.

2. Charles Caldwell Ryrie, *The Ryrie Study Bible* (Chicago: Moody Press, 1978), p. 1817.

3. Ibid.

4. Ibid.

5. William MacDonald, *Enjoying the Proverbs* (Kansas City, KS: Walterick Publishers, 1982), p. 44.

6. John MacArthur, Jr., *The MacArthur New Testament Commentary—1 Timothy* (Chicago: Moody Press, 1995), pp. 80-81.

7. Elizabeth George, *Life Management for Busy Women*, quoting Denis Waitley (Eugene, OR: Harvest House Publishers, 2002), p. 80.

Chapter 15—I Need Help with...My Appetite

1. Elisabeth Elliot, *Discipline, the Glad Surrender* (Grand Rapids: Fleming H. Revell, 1982), pp. 46-47.

2. William MacDonald, *Enjoying the Proverbs* (Kansas City, KS: Walterick Publishers, 1982), p. 126.

3. Derek Kidner, *The Proverbs* (Downer's Grove, IL: InterVarsity Press, 1973), p. 152.

4. Ralph Wardlaw, *Lectures on the Book of Proverbs, Volume III* (Minneapolis, MN: Klock & Klock Christian Publishers, Inc., 1982), p. 91.

5. Ibid., p. 99.

6. Charles R. Swindoll, *The Tale of the Tardy Oxcart*, quoting from *The Strong Family* (Nashville: Word Publishing, 1998), p. 613.

Chapter 16—I Need More Help with...My Appetite

1. D. L. Moody, *Notes from My Bible and Thoughts from My Library* (Grand Rapids: Baker Book House, 1979), p. 269.

2. Curtis Vaughan, *The Old Testament Books of Poetry from 26 Translations* (Grand Rapids: Zondervan Bible Publishers, 1973), pp. 622-23.

3. Robert L. Alden, *Proverbs, A Commentary on an Ancient Book of Timeless Advice* (Grand Rapids: Baker Book House, 1990), p. 208.

4. Robert Jamieson, A.R. Fausset, and David Brown, *Commentary on the Whole Bible* (Grand Rapids: Zondervan Publishing House, 1973), p. 1199.

5. John MacArthur, *The MacArthur Study Bible* (Nashville: Word Publishing, 1997), p. 1737.

6. Moody, *Notes from My Bible*, p. 269.

7. William MacDonald, *Enjoying the Proverbs* (Kansas City, KS: Walterick Publishers, 1982), p. 126.

Chapter 17—I Need Help with...Discipline

1. Both quotes cited from Thomas à Kempis, *The Imitation of Christ—Book 1* (Macon, GA: Mercer University Press, 1989), p. 32.

2. Elisabeth Elliot, *The Shaping of a Christian Family*, quoting an anonymous source (Nashville: Thomas Nelson Publishers, 1991), pp. 95-96.

$\mathcal{I}$f you're benefiting from applying God's great wisdom to your life, you'll want the complementary volume

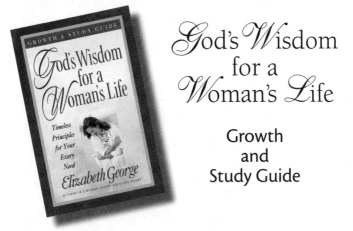

$\mathcal{G}$od's $\mathcal{W}$isdom for a $\mathcal{W}$oman's $\mathcal{L}$ife

Growth and Study Guide

This guide will take you further along the path of growing in God's wisdom. You'll discover many easy-to-do suggestions and highly practical tips for living more wisley in every area of your life—your...

- marriage and family
- home and workplace
- health and ministry
- time and energy
- finances...and more

This growth and study guide is perfect for both personal and group use.

God's Wisdom for a Woman's Life Growth and Study Guide
is available at your local Christian bookstore,
or can be ordered from:

Elizabeth George
P.O. Box 2879
Belfair, WA 98528
Toll-free fax/phone: 1-800-542-4611
www.elizabethgeorge.com

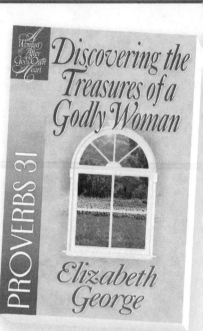

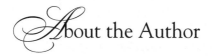# About the Author

Elizabeth George is a bestselling author and speaker whose passion is to teach the Bible in a way that changes women's lives. For information about Elizabeth's books or speaking ministry, to sign up for her mailings, or to share how God has used this book in your life, please write to Elizabeth at:

Elizabeth George
P.O. Box 2879
Belfair, WA 98528

Toll-free fax/phone: 1-800-542-4611
www.elizabethgeorge.com